A Woman
GOD'S SPIRIT
CAN GUIDE

NEW TESTAMENT WOMEN
HELP YOU MAKE
TODAY'S CHOICES

Alice Mathews

 Discovery House.
from Our Daily Bread Ministries

Library of Congress Cataloging-in-Publication Data

Names: Mathews, Alice, 1930– author.
Title: A woman God's Spirit can guide : New Testament women help you make today's choices / Alice Mathews.
Description: Grand Rapids, MI : Discovery House, [2017] | Includes bibliographical references.
Identifiers: LCCN 2017036646 | ISBN 9781627076760 (pbk.)
Subjects: LCSH: Women in the Bible. | Christian women—Religious life.
Classification: LCC BS2445 .M285 2017 | DDC 220.9/2082—dc23
LC record available at https://lccn.loc.gov/2017036646

Printed in the United States of America

First printing in 2017

For all of my former women students
at Gordon-Conwell Theological Seminary
who now carry the torch
for Christ and His Kingdom.
ONWARD!

Contents

Trusting God's Spirit to Guide Us

Have you ever wrestled with how to know "God's will" for your life? Perhaps you heard a teacher or a pastor talk about "being in the center of God's will" or "knowing God's will" but somehow connecting with that and understanding what it really meant eluded you. Perhaps you are wrestling with it right now. You have a big decision to make and feel as if your future hangs in the balance, yet you don't know which choice is best and feel desperate for divine guidance. Or you are searching for your purpose—God's call for you in this season of your life—but aren't sure what you have to offer. Or it may be that you long to experience God's presence and guidance more clearly in the course of the routine decisions you make every day. And now you've pick up a book titled *A Woman God's Spirit Can Guide*, hoping it will shed a bit of light about what it means to be guided by God.

This book was written to help you on that quest. But I have to warn you—you may be surprised by the answers you find. Just as it did with so many biblical characters, God's guidance often leads us into unpredictable circumstances, surprising discoveries, and countercultural choices. If you truly want to be a woman God's Spirit can guide, you can expect the unexpected—but don't fret!

It turns out that God's will isn't a target fifty paces in front of you for which you must carefully aim your one arrow—or you'll miss out entirely. God doesn't play games with us, making his will for us difficult to locate and then nail down. Instead, he invites us into a relationship in which he opens one door now, another door later, and walks with us every step of the way through each one. Furthermore, those doors are different for different women at different times in our lives. So God's will isn't cookie-cutter stuff with just one possible right outcome. That fact can relieve us on one level, but it might frighten us on another level. *What if God's will for my life or the choice God wants me to make is something I don't want? Or something I'm not sure I can do? Or what if it challenges something I've been taught?* The questions and the uncertainty you face may be unsettling, but chances are that they also indicate something very good—God is at work in your life doing a new thing, extending you an invitation to trust him with your questions and with the unknowns.

For example, as you've read the Bible, have you ever come across something in the biblical text that pulls you up short? It was completely unexpected, but there it was on the page. I've had that experience more times than I can count. I've found myself going back over some verses of Scripture again and again, checking to be sure that I hadn't been mistaken. When that happens, it can shake up our preconceptions pretty drastically—and that is a good thing! In a sense, the same dynamic holds true when it comes to finding and following God's will. There is no single script written for all of us, and much of the time, no one right answer for the choices we face. Instead, at such times we discover that

God's Spirit has taken us by the hand and has shown us something we hadn't really thought about before—a new path leading in an unexpected direction.

THE UNEXPECTED WORK OF GOD'S SPIRIT IN AND THROUGH WOMEN

Unexpected direction and surprising discoveries are exactly what I encountered more than twenty-five years ago when I first began to study and teach about women in the Bible. On the pages of Scripture, I discovered women who simply and courageously walked through the doors God opened for them. It was then that I began to envision a series of three books that would explore how biblical women related to the three Persons of the Trinity—Father, Son, and Holy Spirit. This book is the final installment in that series. The first book, *A Woman God Can Use*, was published in 1990 and explores what we can learn from the choices Old Testament women had to make. The second book, *A Woman Jesus Can Teach*, was published in 1991 and focused on the women Jesus encountered and taught as he traveled the dusty roads around Galilee and back and forth to Jerusalem for the great feasts of the Jewish nation. Now that you know the first two books in the series were published more than twenty-five years ago, you may be wondering why it has taken me so long to complete the final installment in the series.

I wanted to write this book back then, but I knew I needed more time to study the biblical texts before opening my laptop and starting to write. If you've been in a situation in which you wondered where God might be leading you but you were bumping up against obstacles to carrying out

God's guidance, you might hesitate, waiting for an open door. That's where I was all those years ago as I studied the women in the New Testament churches for this book. I kept meeting first-century women who were leading in churches in ways that likely would not be affirmed or allowed by some churches today. As I followed the apostle Paul on his various missionary journeys, I also noticed that he often acknowledged and honored women in his letters to various churches. These were women who did unexpected things, who followed God's guidance even when it meant going against the religious and cultural expectations of the day. More than that, these women were recognized leaders.

As we progress through the book, following the women Paul mentions in his letters, we'll take a closer look at the case for women in ministry leadership. Why would we do that in a book about following God's guidance? Because, if we follow the biblical texts, it's simply where a study of women in New Testament churches takes us. If the apostle Paul had no problem with women leaders like Phoebe, Priscilla, or Junia, why should I question how God used them? My study led to their stories in the pages that follow.

Whether we're studying the God we meet in the Old Testament, Jesus in the Gospels, or the Holy Spirit in the rest of the New Testament, we're talking only and always of the triune *God*. So Jesus told his followers in their last meal together before his arrest, death, and resurrection, that he would send them God the Spirit who would continue his work among them, leading them "into all truth" (John 14:17). For them two thousand years ago and for us today, it's the same trustworthy Spirit: we can rely on God's Spirit to teach us what is true as we cope daily with life in a world of falsehoods.

God wants us to know him. That's why Jesus came to earth: to show us the heart of God. In his life and teachings while here on earth, Jesus embodied God's Spirit. We know God because we see God in Jesus. When we study the four Gospels, we learn much about God because of what we see in Jesus. Now Jesus has sent God's Spirit to guide us, to walk with us, to teach us, and then to work through us for Christ and his Kingdom.

But to help us understand how God's guidance works, we have the concrete examples of first-century women guided by God's Spirit in sometimes amazing ways. We don't have to guess at all the ways God's Spirit may be leading us. These first-century women show us some of the many ways in which God's Spirit leads and guides us.

WHAT DOES IT MEAN TO BE A WOMAN GOD'S SPIRIT CAN GUIDE?

God's Spirit (like the wind) moves into our lives and guides us in many different ways. He can guide us through our disabilities as well as our abilities. At times, God's Spirit leads through our circumstances, but other times he opens doors in spite of our circumstances. Still other times, we see an amazing convergence of our concerns and our opportunities that God's Spirit uses to lead us in the path he has for us. And sometimes we just have to keep moving ahead in the dark, trusting that God is leading even when we can't recognize it. In fact, I've found that most of the time I'm more likely to recognize the Spirit's leading in the rear-view mirror of my life. That is, I see God's hand after the fact in ways I wasn't aware of at the time as situations converged to push me in a certain direction. What is important is that whether in the moment or later, I recognize that God's Spirit has been guiding me.

This book is about the many ways God's Spirit led women in the New Testament churches. You may identify with one woman's experience and shake your head about another woman's experience of being guided by the Spirit. That's fine. The point is that God's Spirit treated first-century Christian women as individuals, just as he treats us as individuals today.

What matters most is that God's Spirit is already at work in your life, taking into consideration your unique context, gifts, and resources. Don't miss seeing God's hand in what may look like the ordinary circumstances of your life. You are the object of God's unfailing love, a God who is not far off but is near through the Spirit. God's Spirit wants the very best for you and is always at work to lead and guide you in the right direction. You can trust yourself to God as you watch for those God-sightings in your life that are the mark of the Spirit at work on your behalf.

So what does it mean to be a woman God's Spirit can guide? In the end, it comes down to one thing: when God opens an unexpected door or issues an unexpected invitation, will we say yes? Are we willing to follow wherever God's guidance takes us? The first-century women who became prominent leaders in churches were women who, step by step, said yes to God. That may well be the only thing required to be a woman God's Spirit can guide.

Rest assured that saying yes to God doesn't mean that

we'll find ourselves head-over-heels in something for which we have no ability or interest. God's Spirit always works with who we are as individuals, where we are in life, and what may be a natural next step for us. This is something I know from personal experience.

Years ago, while I was still working with youth in our church, two women invited me to join them in a new outreach ministry to women. At that time, I had no particular interest in working with women, but it was clear that it was time to say yes to that invitation. In the process, I "discovered" women—as well as my lifelong calling. From there, it was step by step, step by step, step by step. I began to learn all I could about women's concerns and obstacles. I learned how to lead Bible studies specifically aimed at women's needs. Then came an opportunity to teach a course on women in a local seminary. As the teaching opportunities expanded, it led me to pursue graduate studies in a doctoral program that led to wider opportunities for ministry to women. Had you told me all those years earlier where that first yes would eventually take me, I would have been dumbfounded. But God's Spirit opens doors for us so naturally that we can say yes to a new challenge without being overwhelmed.

That's how God's Spirit guides us: one step at a time. It's how he guided first-century women who later became leaders in churches. It's how God's Spirit guides us. I'd love to have you join me as we walk with the apostle Paul and others around the Roman Empire in the mid-first century. Some fascinating women were at work for Christ and his Kingdom. Their stories remind us that the Holy Spirit opens doors in surprising places for women willing to say yes to God.

1

Joanna
God's Spirit Uses Difficulties to Guide Us

Dot was my college roommate and best friend. Two years older than I, she modeled a kind of can-do spirit that inspired me even as we did crazy things together, talked deeply about eternal matters, and laughed about human foibles. Dot was petite, but no challenge ever led her to say, "I can't." With hands so small they could hardly stretch an octave on the piano, she could hammer out Rachmaninoff's *Polichinelle* with verve. Once she became convinced that God wanted her to serve as a missionary, she trained in missionary medicine and then earned a pilot's license to fly a plane. After a brief engagement to a college Hulk, she married her childhood best friend, gentle Charles, and they sailed together for East Africa where they planned to spend a lifetime serving in Eritrea.

In time, God gave them a son, but after Mark's birth, Dot—indomitable Dot—found that her muscles wouldn't follow orders. Other symptoms set in, confounding the missionary doctors. Sent to New York for diagnosis, she learned

that she had multiple sclerosis, a disease about which very little was known in the 1950s. Advised to move to Tucson, Arizona, for the dry heat, she and Charles shifted gears and walked away from that missionary dream to a new reality. No longer with a mission agency, they lost that source of income. How could Charles provide for Dot and little Mark? As Dot's disease advanced over the next fifteen years, Charles taught in the public schools while earning a Ph.D., and he eventually became a university history professor. Then on Good Friday in 1971, Dot went to be with Jesus as Charles, a host of other friends, and I mourned the loss of this amazing woman.

We don't understand these twists and turns in life. While Dot's illness dramatically changed the course of their lives, it also eventually led Charles back into church ministry as pastor of a largely Hispanic congregation in Arizona. It wasn't what Dot and Charles had envisioned many years earlier, but through their loss, Charles was still able to live out his calling, and an underserved group of people received pastoral leadership and care from a wise and compassionate shepherd.

Sometimes when we glance into the rearview mirror of life, we can glimpse how God's Spirit has worked through our most difficult experiences to change the course of our lives. That is not to say that God is the author of our suffering or losses. We live in a world shot through with every kind of evil, and the apostle John reminds us that "the world around us is under the control of the evil one" (1 John 5:19). As a result, we suffer from many physical and moral pollutions caused by "the evil one." Yet even illness and loss can be redeemed and used by God to change the direction of our lives for a good purpose.

MEET JOANNA, A JEWISH GIRL WHO MARRIED INTO A ROMAN PALACE

Joanna had likely just turned fourteen when she became a wife. Earlier, her wealthy parents had arranged a good marriage for her to an older man, a non-Jew named Chuza, who served as the business manager to King Herod Antipas. That marriage would move her from the family circle to the king's palace and a life apart from that of most of her Jewish friends. But it would also mean learning Roman ways and probably also learning to speak Greek or Latin rather than the Aramaic she had likely used since early childhood.

Joanna's marriage to Chuza took place in the province of Galilee, a region given to Herod Antipas to rule when his father, King Herod the Great, died in 4 BC (Luke 3:1). Not satisfied with the Jewish towns and cities of Galilee, Antipas decided to build a royal city on a major trade route and near famed hot springs. He also wanted to profit from the burgeoning trade in salted fish from the Sea of Galilee. Choosing the best location near the fishing ports required building over an old Jewish graveyard, but Antipas was undeterred. With its sumptuous palace, its amphitheater for theatrical spectacles, and its Roman baths, the new city, named Tiberias for the Emperor Tiberius, was modeled after the great cities of the Roman Empire. But because of its location over a Jewish cemetery, most devout Jews boycotted the city. Antipas was forced to bring in non-Jews to populate his new capital. We have no evidence that Jesus ever entered Tiberias.

Herod Antipas had married a Nabatean princess to cement relations with the nation on his northern border, but

when he later fell in love with the wife of his half brother, Herod Philip, he divorced his wife and married his sister-in-law. (That divorce cost him a war with his unhappy neighbor to the north.) When John the Baptist spoke out against this illegal marriage, which violated God's law (Leviticus 18:16), Antipas had John the Baptist imprisoned. And when the king was charmed by the sensual dancing of his new wife's daughter, he offered her anything she requested. He then had to acquiesce to her macabre request for John's severed head on a platter.

It was into that palace life that young Joanna moved when she married Chuza, the king's business manager. What do we know about Chuza? Politics likely dictated that this non-Jewish business manager needed a Jewish wife. It was customary in those days for marriages to be arranged within social circles, and it's likely that Joanna came from a Jewish family of wealth and power. She was a perfect fit for the king's finance minister. Joanna likely spent the earliest years of her married life in Roman luxury.

An Illness and a Dramatic Change of Direction

When we look for Joanna in the Bible, we first meet her in the gospel of Luke:

> Jesus began a tour of the nearby towns and villages, preaching and announcing the Good News about the Kingdom of God. He took his twelve disciples with him, along with some women who had been cured of evil spirits and diseases. Among them were Mary Magdalene, from whom he had cast out seven demons; *Joanna, the wife of Chuza, Herod's business manager*; Susanna; and many others who

were contributing from their own resources to support Jesus and his disciples. (LUKE 8:1–3, emphasis added)

What? An aristocratic woman from King Antipas's palace is touring with Jesus, his male disciples, and some other women? How could this be? Then we notice that Joanna is included among women who had been cured of either a physical disease or a disease of the soul. In Luke 8, we have no further facts about her. We do not learn the nature of her illness or how she came to be healed. Nor do we have any information in the Bible about the time lapse between her marriage to Chuza and the onset of this debilitating illness. It could have been a number of years. Luke simply tells us that she was now part of the Jesus band, going from town to town as Jesus preached the Good News of God's Kingdom.

Think about the huge social gulf Joanna had to cross as she moved from the Herodian upper class of Tiberias, the royal city of the Roman king, to trekking from town to town with Jesus, listening to him teach and watching him heal the sick. Accustomed to palace life and its luxurious amenities, she nevertheless chose to live as part of a ragtag band of fishermen and others. And there is a reasonably good chance she wouldn't have found a warm welcome among them. As part of the alien Roman aristocracy, hated by most Galileans for the heavy taxes Antipas imposed and the Roman pagan approach to all of life, she might well have been considered "the enemy." But she risked that because she had met her Savior. She realized that Jesus's power to heal was from God whose Kingdom he announced. It was an upside-down Kingdom, contrary to all she knew about palaces and kings and royal rule. He talked about loving not just your own kind, but also about loving your enemies. He was hard on religious elites, but tender toward those with a contrite spirit. There was also quite a bit about this Kingdom of God that had to do with renouncing status and wealth rather than parading it as proof of God's favor.

Joanna had been a wealthy aristocratic woman in a land of poor and oppressed people. Imagine the risk she took when she crossed over from her elite circle to become one with ordinary folks—those with whom Jesus associated. British New Testament scholar Richard Bauckham notes that for Joanna, "throwing her lot with Jesus was a radical conversion to the poor."[1] Had it not been for the incurable illness that first drove her to find that Jewish miracle-worker she had heard about, Joanna may have never left her comfortable life in the king's palace. But through her illness, God led her to Jesus. It is the same for us: God's Spirit can use our most difficult challenges to lead us in new and unexpected directions.

THE COMPLEX LIVES OF WOMEN IN FIRST-CENTURY ISRAEL

In the Ancient Near East, women were often sequestered in their homes and kept out of sight. Why? In the legalistic Judaism practiced by the scribes and Pharisees in New Testament times, women were often considered inherently dangerous and corrupt, responsible for the evil in the world because Eve had initiated eating the forbidden fruit (Genesis 3:6). Never mind that Adam joined in the feast on the forbidden fruit with no hesitation![2]

By first-century moral standards, when women were outside their homes, they were considered to be little more than a sexual temptation to men. For that reason, some Pharisees were so intent on having no contact with a woman that they would not greet even their own mother if they saw her on the street. In fact, one group of Pharisees was known as "the Bleeding Ones" because they walked around with their eyes closed to keep from seeing a woman in public even from a distance. As a result, they would crash into walls and suffer cuts and bruises. Their resultant bleeding was a mark of their superior moral refusal to be tempted by the sight of a woman.

In addition to being sequestered and deemed a moral threat, women were also considered unworthy of learning God's law. Rabbi Eliezer had declared, "If any man gives his daughter a knowledge of the Law, it is as though he taught her lechery" (m. Sota 3:4). Jose ben Johnan of Jerusalem had taught, "He who talks much with womankind brings evil upon himself and neglects the study of the Law and at the last will inherit Gehenna" (m. Abot. 1:5). In the eyes of many Jews, teaching a woman Mosaic law was not only unnecessary; it was downright wrong.

In light of such malign attitudes toward women, we may be shocked to learn that some women traveled all around Galilee as part of Jesus's band. Were they bold or simply reckless? How did God's Spirit guide and influence their stunning choices? How is it that they seem to be respected rather than ostracized by their communities? And how did their humble and courageous choice alter their lives?

The women we meet in Luke 8 were far more complex than we sometimes think. What was true for some women was not true for others, and these women could travel publicly with Jesus and his disciples because of who they were—women of means and privilege. Luke tells us that Mary Magdalene, Joanna, Susanna, and many other women "were contributing from their own resources to support Jesus and his disciples" (Luke 8:3). These were women who had access to wealth and were in a position to contribute generously to Jesus.

Luke tells us that their attachment to Jesus grew out of what he had already done for them: he had healed them. Their gratitude to him led to their decision to use their resources to fund his ministry. So we find these women traveling with Jesus and his male disciples on his tours of the towns and villages near the Sea of Galilee. Did tongues wag? Were the townspeople scandalized? To understand how these women were able to travel with Jesus and his band without scandal or community criticism, we need to know a bit about "benefaction" and how it shielded bene-factors from public disapproval in the first century.

New Testament scholar Lynn Cohick tells us that bene-faction was gender blind. This allowed a woman to move about freely in public if what she did contributed to the common good. Because Jesus was healing multitudes, these women were making that possible by supporting him finan-cially in his work. Joanna's social position allowed her to travel freely with Jesus because her financial support was enabling a good thing benefitting so many poorer folks.

But Joanna's presence with the band might have had another benefit. When we read the early chapters of the gospels by Matthew, Mark, or Luke, we note that every-one was gossiping about this amazing miracle worker, Jesus. Huge crowds followed him wherever he went, and he was kept busy day and night healing the sick and casting demons out of afflicted people. News of him was on everyone's lips, and even King Antipas was curious and wanted to see Jesus at work (Luke 23:8). While early on many of the scribes and Pharisees condemned Jesus for his actions and teachings, his good works throughout the towns and villages in Galilee protected him from the wrath of those religious leaders. Joanna's connection to the Jesus band may also have garnered the group some protection even from the palace.

But Jesus didn't stay only in Galilee. Each year, he made the journey down to Jerusalem in Judea for one of the great feasts of the nation. It was there that the Jewish religious leaders could scheme for a means of seeing Jesus dead. Not only the twelve disciples but also this band of women accompanied Jesus on those treks to Jerusalem. The story of his last trip to Jerusalem takes up much space in each of the four Gospels. In John's Gospel, for example, two-thirds of the book (from chapter 7:10 through chapter 20) detail those last days of teaching in Jerusalem, then Jesus's arrest, his trial, his crucifixion, and finally his resurrection.

Joanna was part of that group to the end. We find her watching Jesus die on Golgotha (Mark 15:41). Had you been in her situation, what might you have felt at that time? With the other women, she had invested her resources in his ministry, but now he was dying on a cross. He had rescued them from debilitating diseases. He had taught them the way to God. He had given them hope for God's Kingdom. But now? Joanna and the other women could do nothing but watch the slow, agonizing death of their Lord.

But even in his death, these women had one more ministry to perform: his body must be anointed properly. It would be risky. In fact, doing so might well incur the wrath of

Jerusalem's Roman governor. But it had to be done—and they *wanted* to do it. Their love for Jesus compelled them to give his body a proper burial. Luke tells us:

> As his body was taken away, the women from Galilee followed and saw the tomb where his body was placed. Then they went home and prepared spices and ointments to anoint his body. But by the time they were finished the Sabbath had begun, so they rested as required by the law. (LUKE 23:55–56)

Then before dawn, the morning after the Sabbath had ended, these women were on their way back to the tomb to complete the task before them.

They faced what seemed to be an impossible situation. The Jewish religious leaders had insisted that the tomb be sealed and a Roman guard posted in front of it so that the followers of Jesus could not steal the body and insist that Jesus was once again alive. How would these women deal with that sealed cave and the Roman soldiers? That was their dilemma.

But these women were determined! Nothing, including the potential threats and unknown obstacles before them, could keep them from that sealed tomb. Who were the women bent on this dangerous mission? Combining lists from the four gospels, we know that the group included Mary of Magdala; Joanna, the wife of Chuza, Herod's steward; Susanna; Mary the mother of Jesus; Mary the wife of Clopas; Mary the mother of James; Mary the mother of Joses; and the mother of Zebedee's sons. Except for Mary Magdalene and Susanna, all of these women were married and most were mothers of adult sons. Of all the witnesses to the crucifixion, they were most constant throughout Jesus's suffering and death. They were last at the cross and the tomb, and first as witnesses to Jesus's resurrection.

LAST AT THE TOMB, FIRST TO ANNOUNCE JESUS'S RESURRECTION

Luke reports what happened next:

> Very early on Sunday morning the women went to the tomb, taking the spices they had prepared. They found that the stone had been rolled away from the entrance. So they went in, but they didn't find the body of the Lord Jesus. As they stood there puzzled, two men suddenly appeared to them, clothed in dazzling robes.
>
> The women were terrified and bowed with their faces to the ground. Then the men asked, "Why are you looking among the dead for someone who is alive? He isn't here! He is risen from the dead! Remember what he told you back in Galilee, that the Son of Man must be betrayed into the hands of sinful men and be crucified, and that he would rise again on the third day."
>
> Then they remembered that he had said this. So they rushed back from the tomb to tell his eleven disciples—and everyone else—what had happened. It was Mary Magdalene, *Joanna*, Mary the mother of James, and several other women who told the apostles what had happened. But the story sounded like nonsense to the men, so they didn't believe it. (LUKE 24:1–11, emphasis added)

Because these women had not flinched in the face of danger, they became the first to announce the resurrection of Jesus to his disciples—most of whom had fled the scene of his trial and crucifixion, fearing that they would be the next to die a brutal death. Reading the final chapters of each of the Gospels, we see how difficult it was for the eleven disciples—those closest to Jesus throughout his ministry—to comprehend what had really happened. After his resurrection, in appearance after appearance at meals behind locked doors, or out in the open by the seaside, Jesus repeatedly commented on how slow they were to believe what their eyes could plainly see. Here is how Luke describes one such encounter:

> The whole group was startled and frightened, thinking they were seeing a ghost!
>
> "Why are you frightened?" [Jesus] asked. "Why are your hearts filled with doubt? Look at my hands. Look at my feet. You can see that it's really me. Touch me and make sure that I am not a ghost, because ghosts don't have bodies, as you see that I do." . . . Still they stood there in disbelief, filled with joy and wonder. (LUKE 24:37–39, 41)

Not so with the women who had followed Jesus from Galilee, Joanna among them. And God rewarded their fidelity with proof positive from the angels who instructed them at the empty tomb. What was the source of their fidelity? In every case, these women had a personal experience of God's love and grace through the actions of God's Son, Jesus. For Joanna and others, it was the healing touch that delivered them from debilitating illness. In the words of an old chorus sung in churches back in the 1950s,

> *"How can I do less*
> *than give him my best*
> *and live for him completely,*
> *After all he's done for me?"*

Touched by God's grace, these women never wavered in their commitment to Jesus's welfare in both life and death. Their reward was to become the first evangelists, the first to announce Jesus's resurrection and the grace of God this would provide to all who believe in him.

Jesus's story moves on. After forty days appearing here and there (at one point, to more than five hundred of his followers at a single time, as recorded 1 Corinthians 15:6), Jesus commissioned his followers with these words:

> "I have been given all authority in heaven and on earth. Therefore, go and make disciples of all the nations, baptizing them in the name of the Father and the Son and the Holy Spirit. Teach these new disciples to obey all the commands I have given you. And be sure of this: I am with you always, even to the end of the age." (MATTHEW 28:18–20)

In his last time with his followers, he promised them,

> "You will receive power when the Holy Spirit comes upon you. And you will be my witnesses, telling people about me everywhere—in Jerusalem, throughout Judea, in Samaria, and to the ends of the earth." (ACTS 1:8)

As they watched, Jesus was taken up into a cloud so they could no longer see him. Returning to Jerusalem and to the upstairs room where they had been staying, "they all met together and were constantly united in prayer, along with Mary the mother of Jesus, several other women, and the brothers of Jesus" (Acts 1:14).

Note that the women had not returned to Galilee to pick up their former lives. They had not disappeared. They were faithful to Jesus's final instructions—to remain in Jerusalem until God's Spirit had come upon them for ministry. The growing group, now numbering 120, prayed earnestly for this. Acts 2 describes the scene in that upstairs room:

> On the day of Pentecost all the believers were meeting together in one place. Suddenly, there was a sound from heaven like the roaring of a mighty windstorm, and it filled the house where they were sitting. Then, what looked like flames or tongues of fire appeared and settled on each of them. And everyone present was filled with the Holy Spirit. (ACTS 2:1–4)

Luke is clear that all 120 men and women in that room were filled by the Holy Spirit. They then poured out into the streets of Jerusalem with the astounding news about Jesus.

We don't hear about most of these women again, nor do we hear of most of the original male disciples. The story of the early church shifts to Peter, and then to Paul throughout the rest of the New Testament. But if we continue reading in Acts 2, we learn that as each one was filled with the Holy Spirit, he or she "began speaking in other languages, as the Holy Spirit gave them this ability" (v. 2:4). Why? For a very important reason!

Pentecost was one of the three major Jewish feasts each year, and Jews from all over the known world made the trip to Jerusalem for the celebrations. Jerusalem in the first century was a relatively small city with no more than 55,000 residents. But at the time of the great feasts, the incoming pilgrims more than tripled the population to around 180,000. God's timing was perfect!

> At that time there were devout Jews from every nation living in Jerusalem. When they heard the loud noise, everyone

came running, and they were bewildered to hear their own languages being spoken by the believers.

They were completely amazed. "How can this be?" they exclaimed. "These people are all from Galilee, and yet we hear them speaking in our own native languages! Here we are—Parthians, Medes, Elamites, people from Mesopotamia, Judea, Cappadocia, Pontus, the province of Asia, Phrygia, Pamphylia, Egypt and the areas of Libya around Cyrene, visitors from Rome (both Jews and converts to Judaism), Cretans, and Arabs. And we all hear these people speaking in our own languages about the wonderful things God has done!" (ACTS 2:5–11)

Little Jerusalem was packed with people from every part of the known world. Only on one of the three great pilgrimage feasts of the Jewish year would the city have had such an audience for the sermon Peter preached about Jesus. A week earlier or a week later, the town would have shrunk to its normal population. But not at Pentecost! The whole world had representatives who could hear that Good News in their own language. The Galilean women were part of that proclamation band, gifted by God's Spirit to spread the word about Jesus to those who would carry it thousands of miles as they returned home.

GOD'S SPIRIT AT WORK

How did God's Spirit lead Joanna and the other women? In their case, God began with their clear and obvious need. Each of them had some kind of disease from which they needed to be healed. Jesus met their need and cured them. For Joanna, Jesus not only changed her physically, but his life and teachings changed her emotionally and spiritually, giving her new values and a new purpose in life.

In response to the grace these women received from Jesus, they left the comfort of their well-to-do homes to travel with and minister to him throughout Galilee and back and forth to Jerusalem for the great Jewish feasts. When the disciples fled for fear of the Jewish religious leaders, the women remained visible and constant—at the cross, at the tomb, and after Jesus's resurrection and ascension. For their fidelity they were included in that first band of Spirit-filled men and women who shared the Good News with folks who would carry it to the ends of their known world.

Imagine the giant step of faith Joanna took when she left a palace to travel around the Galilean countryside with a ragtag band of fishermen and hangers-on. Can you fathom the gap between her former life and the one she chose as a follower of Jesus? Accustomed to fine foods, costly clothing, and servants to carry out her every wish, she nevertheless embraced a new life of service to others. But for her, this step led to a richness no palace could provide. In the beginning of her walk with Jesus, she could not know what opportunities or challenges might lie ahead. We'll meet Joanna again later in this book, in a life that carried her beyond her wildest imaginings. In Galilee, she knew only that she had met the Savior of the world and he had forever changed her life.

God's Spirit often uses our deep needs as a springboard to guide us into the new life we can have in Jesus Christ. When we experience that new life, we respond with love and gratitude, just as the women did who traveled with Jesus. Like them, we want to serve God's Kingdom with whatever gifts we've been given. For most of us, embracing a life of service will likely not require a change as dramatic as the one Joanna experienced. But when God's Spirit guides us, we often do end up going through doors of opportunity that take us by surprise. In the process, we discover gifts within ourselves we had no idea we possessed. Or we become aware of opportunities we would not have considered earlier. We find ourselves in situations that astonish us with their new possibilities. When that happens, we can be assured that it is God at work, guiding us into new avenues of service for our Lord. Who knows what that door of opportunity might be for you?

• • •

QUESTIONS FOR INDIVIDUAL REFLECTION
OR GROUP DISCUSSION

1. What stands out most to you about the story of Joanna and the other women in Jesus's band? In what ways does their story encourage you or challenge you?

2. How do you respond to the idea that God's Spirit uses our difficulties to guide us? Overall, is it an idea that you find distressing or comforting? Why?

3. In what ways, if any, would you say God's Spirit has used past difficulties to guide you? What unforeseen opportunities or growth did you experience as a result?

4. In what ways might God's Spirit be using any current difficulties to guide you in this season of life—to draw you closer to Jesus, to grow your faith and gifts, or to open new opportunities for service?

2

Dorcas

God's Spirit Uses Our Abilities to Guide Us

As a teenager who had grown up in the church, my burning question was, "How can I find out God's will for my life?" I was not alone with that question. In our youth group, while we seldom got much useful help on that issue from our leaders, it was the subject a lot of us talked about without them. It seemed that so much depended on the answer! To us, these felt like life-or-death questions: *What should I major in when I go to college? Are there things I should be doing right now to help prepare for that future? What if God's will for me turns out to be something I hate? What if God's will is such a narrow slice of life that I could miss it and be doomed?* I wanted to use my abilities in ways that would count for God's purposes. But how could I be sure I was on the right track?

What I've since learned is that we didn't need to be so afraid about somehow missing God's will. We've been wired by God with gifts and abilities that in one way or another and at the right time will open the right doors for us. Our task may well be simply to hone those gifts as we're given opportunity. In the process, we trust God to guide us to use those gifts for divine purposes.

HOW A JEWISH SEAMSTRESS NAMED DORCAS DISCERNED GOD'S WILL

Go with me in your imagination to a small seaside town in Israel called Joppa. Its claim to fame was that it was one of the oldest functioning harbors in the world. If you remember the Old Testament story of Jonah, it was from this harbor that he boarded a large cargo ship that would take him as far from God's will as he could possibly get (Jonah 1:3). But in New Testament times, Joppa's harbor primarily served the town's many fishermen. And because the Mediterranean Sea could be rough sailing for those who made their living on it, Joppa lost many of those fishermen, leaving behind widows and orphans.

It's in Joppa that we meet a kind woman who has two names: Tabitha and Dorcas. Tabitha, her Aramaic name, is how the apostle Peter addressed her, because both of them lived in Israel and spoke Aramaic. But Luke, writing his account of the early church (the Acts of the Apostles), called her by her Greek name, Dorcas. Luke was a Gentile, not a Jew, and he wrote both the Gospel of Luke and the Acts of the Apostles to a Greek man named Theophilus. Eventually, both books were directed to primarily gentile audiences. Today, this double-name thing would be similar to referring to Peter as "Pedro" when speaking to a Hispanic listener. Same person, different names in different languages. "Tabitha" (in Aramaic) and "Dorcas" (in Greek) both mean the same thing: "gazelle," a small, graceful, soft-eyed antelope.

So we meet Tabitha/Dorcas in Luke's letter to Theophilus: "There was a believer in Joppa named Tabitha (which in Greek is Dorcas)" (Acts 9:36). The English word *believer* doesn't capture the richness of the Greek word Luke used to describe her. He identified her as *mathetria*, the Greek word for a female disciple, an avid learner. Dorcas did more than just give intellectual assent to the Christian message; she learned all she could about Jesus's life and teachings and then put that learning into solid action. How did that show up in her life?

Luke continues: "She was always doing kind things for others and helping the poor." What kind of "kind things" did she do for others? She used her skills as a seamstress to clothe them. When she unexpectedly died, we learn that "the room was filled with widows who were weeping and showing [Peter] the coats and other clothes Dorcas had made for them" (Acts 9:39). Dorcas was a *doer*. She cared about the practical needs of those who were too poor to provide for themselves.

Dorcas held in her hand a sewing needle and in her heart a deep concern and passion for the poor and for widows in Joppa. Using her abilities and passion, God's Spirit led her directly to an opportunity—to use her needle to address a serious problem in her community.

But let's go back to her untimely death. Here is how Luke tells the story:

> About this time she became ill and died. Her body was washed for burial and laid in an upstairs room. But the

believers had heard that Peter was nearby at Lydda, so they sent two men to beg him, "Please come as soon as possible!"

So Peter returned with them; and as soon as he arrived, they took him to the upstairs room. The room was filled with widows who were weeping and showing him the coats and other clothes Dorcas had made for them. But Peter asked them all to leave the room; then he knelt and prayed. Turning to the body he said, "Get up, Tabitha." And she opened her eyes! When she saw Peter, she sat up! He gave her his hand and helped her up. Then he called in the widows and all the believers, and he presented her to them alive.

The news spread through the whole town, and many believed in the Lord. And Peter stayed a long time in Joppa, with Simon, a tanner of hides. (ACTS 9:37–43)

What a dramatic scene that was! And note the result: not only was Dorcas restored to life, but as word of this miracle spread through Joppa, "many believed in the Lord."

It is clear from the text that Dorcas's commitment to the widows' needs was not a part-time hobby. She did much more than simply make an occasional donation of used clothing. She lived to care for those around her who needed what she could give. She knew that providing clothing for these folks allowed her to carry out Jesus's teaching: "When you [were doing good] to one of the least of these my brothers and sisters, you were doing it to me" (Matthew 25:40). Dorcas was a genuine *mathetria*, an eager and enthusiastic disciple who lived out all that she learned from Jesus.

What drove Dorcas to use her time and resources to serve her community? We don't know all the ways in which God prepared her for her ministry. But as a committed follower of Jesus Christ, she was most likely acquainted with the Scriptures read each week in the synagogue. Perhaps her heart had been stirred when God's Word admonished her to "Judge fairly, and show mercy and kindness to one another. Do not oppress widows, orphans, foreigners and the poor. And do not scheme against each other" (Zechariah 7:9–10). It's also possible that she might have heard James preach, saying, "Pure and genuine religion in the sight of God the Father means caring for orphans and widows in their distress and refusing to let the world corrupt you" (James 1:27).

What else do we know about Dorcas? Because the text never mentions a husband, some speculate that she herself was a widow, though we can't confirm that. Others speculate that she might have been poor, but that is unlikely. She had a house with an upstairs room, something only a person with wealth could afford. If she had been poor, it's also unlikely that she would have had the means to secure fabrics from which to make clothing.

What we can say is that the widows who showed her work to Peter considered her a beloved friend. Their presence in that upstairs room shows their familiarity with her home and probably with her ongoing hospitality. It's possible that her home may even have been a meeting place for the local church, though this is not stated in Acts. We do know that many women in the New Testament, once they became followers of Jesus, subsequently opened their homes as a meeting place for local believers. The text tells us that she was very kind to those in need, perhaps giving them more than just the clothes she made for them. With her warm heart and listening ear, she no doubt also gave them the dignity and respect that others in the community likely denied them. Whatever else she gave them, it was always the fruit of her ability to sew that tangibly served her community.

But again, most of what we know comes from speculation rather than documentation. We know for sure only what Luke actually tells us in Acts 9. Her name and her work are familiar to us because God's Spirit led Luke to include her story in Acts. Behind that lies an interesting fact from the British New Testament scholar Richard Bauckham. He reminds us that the four Gospels and Luke's book of Acts were all written decades after Jesus's death, resurrection, and ascension. So whenever we come across the name of a man or woman in those books, it means that he or she was already well-known to the gentile Christians scattered across the Roman Empire. We know Dorcas's name because a couple decades after her death and return to life, her name and work were kept alive as a model for new Christians to follow in the churches founded by Paul, Peter, and others.

Discerning God's Will from Dorcas's Example

We could say that Dorcas knew God's will for her life by what was in her hand—she was clearly a gifted seamstress. Nevertheless, it would have been easy for her to feel overwhelmed or maybe even inadequate in the face of such great needs in her community. If so, perhaps she heard a whisper of God's reassurance, *You already have everything you need to do what I'm asking you to do. If you'll trust me, I will use you.* If there was any reluctance, she soon overcame it and then put her abilities into action. But acknowledging her skill with a needle stops short of all that she models for us. From her, we also learn two other necessary pieces that help us discern how God's Spirit guides us.

In addition to her skill, Dorcas cared deeply about her community. Why else would she devote herself to endless sewing projects to clothe orphans and widows in Joppa? She had a passion to meet their needs. Married to that needle in her hand was also a deep, driving concern for the women and children who shivered without adequate clothes.

Dorcas was also in a place in which the needs of her community were obvious. With so many men lost at sea each year, Joppa's widows and orphans could not be ignored. For this godly seamstress, the need was everywhere evident. She didn't need to spend a lot of time fretfully wondering or discerning what it was God might want her to do. The responsibility to do something to alleviate the suffering of those around her was inescapable.

So from Dorcas we learn that God's Spirit guides us, not only through what is in our hand (our available skills, gifts, resources), but also through the passion in our hearts and the opportunities before us. It takes all three working together to whisper in our soul the course of action we should take.

There is a New Testament story of Peter and John that beautifully illustrates these principles we learn from Dorcas about discerning God's will. Remember the story of Pentecost, when God's Spirit had come upon the 120 followers of Jesus who had gathered in an upstairs room in Jerusalem? The first evidence of the Spirit's work in their lives was that the thousands of pilgrims from every part of the known world miraculously heard the story of Jesus in their own language.

As the apostle Peter preached to these thousands of people (three thousand of them became followers of Jesus that day), he cited the Old Testament prophet Joel:

> "In the last days," God says, "I will pour out my Spirit upon all people. Your sons and daughters will prophesy. Your young men will see visions, and your old men will dream dreams. In those days I will pour out my Spirit even on my servants—men and women alike—and they will prophesy. And I will cause wonders in the heavens above and signs on the earth below. . . . But everyone who calls on the name of the LORD will be saved." (ACTS 2:17–19, 21)

Men and women alike would receive God's Spirit to both guide and empower them.

Then, just days after the feast of Pentecost as Peter and John were on their way to the temple to pray, they passed a beggar who had been lame from birth. Note carefully what Peter said in response when the beggar asked the two men for money:

> "I don't have any silver or gold for you. But I'll give you what I have. In the name of Jesus Christ the Nazarene, get up and walk!"
>
> Then Peter took the lame man by the right hand and helped him up. And as he did, the man's feet and ankles were instantly healed and strengthened. (ACTS 3:6–7)

What did Peter have in his hand? He had something far better than money. He had the experience of three years spent with Jesus—a time in which he had been taught and transformed. Now empowered by the Holy Spirit, Peter was fully equipped for the healing and teaching work God had called him to. And he freely gave what God had given him.

So when we come to Acts 9, back to that upstairs room filled with grieving widows, we are not surprised that God's Spirit again led Peter as he called Dorcas back to life for the benefit of those for whom she cared. This wasn't a miracle just for the sake of having a miracle. It was God's specific action for the sake of the community to which Dorcas selflessly ministered. She took seriously God's commands about the most vulnerable people in the town—the poor and the widows.

God calls each of us to be concerned about the marginalized—the poor, the disabled, the aged, the homeless, and children without families—and to care for them. And when we make God's concern for these people our concern, we show folks around us the heart of God. The psalmist reminds us of God's tender heart for those who are suffering:

> The LORD opens the eyes of the blind. The LORD lifts up those who are weighed down. The LORD loves the godly. The LORD protects the foreigners among us. He cares for the orphans and widows, but he frustrates the plans of the wicked. (PSALM 146:8–9)

That is God's heart. Knowing that, Dorcas was God's instrument to the poor and the widows in Joppa.

God's Spirit often guides us by what is in our hand. The women in Luke 8 had wealth in their hands and used it to finance Jesus's ministry in Galilee. Dorcas had a needle in her hand and used it to make warm clothing for those who might otherwise have had nothing but rags to wear.

Peter had no money in his hand, but he had three years' experience of traveling with Jesus. He had been empowered by God to cure the sick and raise the dead to life again

(Matthew 10:8). Joanna, Dorcas, Peter—each used what God had placed in their hands. That is how God's Spirit guided each one of them. And that may well be how God will guide us.

WHAT HAS GOD PUT INTO MY HAND?

God's Spirit could lead Dorcas because she had the skill. She had the passion. She had the opportunity. Today, we have a far greater range of opportunities than did women in first-century Palestine. But the question we must ask ourselves remains the same: *What has God put into my hand?* And then, *How am I using it?* No two people will answer those questions the same way. One woman may have specialized training that equips her to work in a field that meets human needs. Another woman might have a mixing bowl, a skillet, and a good stove. God's Spirit guides her to use her culinary skills to feed people in need. For still another woman, it may be a reliable automobile and available time to take a disabled or elderly neighbor to a grocery store or doctor's appointment. Still another woman may have a heart for neighborhood children who need more love or guidance than they receive at home. For yet another woman, it could simply be a compassionate ear and a loving touch that assure hurting people that someone cares about them. For Dorcas, it was a needle. As a faithful follower of Jesus, she used that needle to meet the needs of the poor.

As you look around you, what needs do you see? What has God put in your hand that could help you to meet that need? When your ability, your passion, and your opportunity all come together, you can move forward with confidence.

The God who created you has uniquely equipped you to know and to do his will. You don't have to worry that you might miss it. Your God-given abilities and passions will open doors of opportunity for you to serve in God-honoring ways. That is God's will for your life.

What has God put in your hand? God's Spirit often guides simply and directly: he uses what you have in your hand.

• • •

QUESTIONS FOR PERSONAL REFLECTION OR GROUP DISCUSSION

1. When you first became a Christian, what was your understanding of what it meant to discern God's will for your life? For example, did you think it was simple and obvious? Were you afraid you might miss it? How has your understanding changed over time?

2. Dorcas probably didn't have to search very far to discern what God's will for her was. She simply had to make a connection between her abilities and passions and the needs and opportunities around her. In what ways, if any, do you relate to Dorcas's experience? When have you felt that God's will for you in a particular situation was clear and simply required your response? How did you respond?

3. If someone were to ask you about your abilities and passions, what would you say? How would you describe them?

4. As you reflect on your abilities and your passions, how might you respond if God were to say to you, *You already have everything you need to do what I'm asking you to do. If you'll trust me, I will use you?*

3

The Hungry Greek Widows
God's Spirit Guides Us
through Negative Examples

From 1941 until 1945, World War II engaged virtually the whole world. The United States had joined others in the Allied cause, fighting fascist Germany and Italy in Europe and Japan in Asia. As my government rounded up and interred all second- and third-generation Japanese living peacefully in the country, the media whipped up hatred for anyone with a German or Japanese name. Just a few houses down on our street, some cruel neighborhood boys tied the young son of a German immigrant to a tree and left him there for several hours because any German must be the "enemy." Until that time, I didn't know the word "racism," but it was a reality people all around me suffered.

My hometown, Detroit, was called the "Arsenal of Democracy" as automobile factories were retrofitted to make planes, tanks, and other instruments of war. When military conscription took men out of the factories and made them soldiers, the manpower shortage was great, and 350,000 people poured into the city from impoverished parts of the nation to take the thousands of available post-Depression jobs.

How does a city assimilate and house the rapid arrival of so many newcomers? Although only 14 percent of the new arrivals were African-American, they were excluded from all-white neighborhoods and from all public housing except the Brewster-Douglass housing projects. Many had to live in homes without indoor plumbing and they paid rents double or more than the amount paid by families in white districts. Racism was alive and well—and blatant.

In June 1943, racial tensions in Detroit were high, especially among whites who felt that African-Americans threatened their jobs, their homes, and their way of life. A fistfight in a park between black and white teens quickly spread into a three-day riot in which thirty-four people were killed.

Racism even reared its ugly head within my small circle of close friends. I spent most of my free time with four girlfriends: Joanie, Janie, Jeano, and Monica. Joanie and Janie were Jewish, which was fine with me because Jesus and his disciples were Jews. One weekend, Janie and I were visiting Jeano, whose parents belonged to the posh local boat club. Jeano's mother asked her to stop by the club with a message for her dad, so the three of us went on that errand. When we arrived at the impressive staircase outside the club, Jeano said I could come in with her, but Janie would have to stay outside because Jews weren't allowed in the club. I chose to stay with Janie while Jeano delivered her message. That was the year I learned that a lot of people hated Jews, and I was struck by the injustice of such hatred—hatred (and fear) of anyone different. Looking back, I realize it was also when I began to see how God could use a negative experience like racism to help me grasp God's love for the whole world of people, some like me and some very unlike me.

RACISM AMONG CHRISTIANS?

Racism isn't something new in our lifetime. It is a vile malady that has infected the world almost from the beginning of time. So it shouldn't come as a big surprise that it was rampant in the first century AD and that it showed up even among the new Christians in Jerusalem. In Acts 6, we learn that "as the believers rapidly multiplied, there were rumblings of discontent. The Greek-speaking believers complained about the Hebrew-speaking believers, saying that their widows were being discriminated against in the daily distribution of food" (Acts 6:1–3).

One result of Pentecost was that "all the believers met together in one place and shared everything they had. They . . . shared their meals with joy and great generosity—all the while praising God and enjoying the goodwill of all the people" (Acts 2:44, 46–47). What had happened between that happy beginning in Acts 2 and the Greeks' complaints in Acts 6? How is it that what had begun so joyfully and generously should in a relatively short time lead to short-changing some believers' food allotments based on their race?

The early chapters of Acts detail the birth pangs of the Christian community based in Jerusalem. At that time, the people in Palestine were under the heel of the Roman Empire, and numerous dissident groups of Jews hoped and worked for a dismantling of Roman power. In fact, on several occasions, Jesus in his earthly ministry had to counter pressure to become that charismatic leader who would deliver the Jews from Roman occupation. It was disappointment with his insistence that God's Kingdom was spiritual, not military, that led some to turn away from him (John 6:66). Jewish aspirations for their own powerful kingdom on earth, a kingdom that could defeat the powers of Rome, led to several fierce but unsuccessful rebellions in the first century.

Meanwhile, the Christian community in Jerusalem grew rapidly, including Gentile as well as Jewish members. These early Gentiles were converts first to Judaism, then to Christianity. But for some Jewish Christians, if these "Greeks" did not support their aspirations for freedom from Rome, they were also "the enemy."

You may remember from Acts 2:9–11, that those who responded to Peter's sermon at Pentecost represented ethnic groups from every part of the known world—Jews in their faith, but otherwise ethnically diverse. So it's not surprising that we read "there were rumblings of discontent" among the Greek-speaking believers who felt their widows were being discriminated against by the Hebrew-speaking believers. In a very short time, the fledgling church went from a deep sense of awe as they shared everything they had, to division and discrimination.

GOD'S POSITION ON THIS ISSUE

We might be tempted to attribute the racism of some in the early church to ignorance or to the unenlightened culture of the day. However, we must not forget that the new Christian community had its ethical roots deep in God's revealed will in the Old Testament, including passages like this:

"For the LORD your God . . . shows no partiality and cannot be bribed. He ensures that orphans and widows receive justice. He shows love to the foreigners living among you and gives them food and clothing. So you, too, must show love to foreigners, for you yourselves were once foreigners in the land of Egypt." (DEUTERONOMY 10:17–19)

In case the Hebrew Christians missed it that time, God came back to the same theme again: "True justice must be given to foreigners living among you and to orphans, and you must never accept a widow's garment as security for her debt" (Deuteronomy 24:17). Moses even set up a responsive worship ritual in which the Levites (the priestly class) would shout, "Cursed is anyone who denies justice to foreigners, orphans, or widows," and all the people would reply, "Amen" (Deuteronomy 27:19). When God himself levels the severity of a curse against those who would deny "justice to foreigners, orphans, or widows," it's clear he means business. Treating orphans, widows, or foreigners equitably wasn't just a suggestion or a nice idea. It was central to how God expected his people to think, to act, and to live.

When the ancient Israelites disregarded God's clear commands, he raised up prophets to call his straying people to repentance. Listen to the prophet Isaiah speak God's truth to these sinful Israelites:

"Though you offer many prayers, I will not listen, for your hands are covered with the blood of innocent victims. Wash yourselves and be clean! Get your sins out of my sight. Give up your evil ways. Learn to do good. Seek justice. Help the oppressed. Defend the cause of orphans. Fight for the rights of widows." (ISAIAH 1:15–17)

Later, the prophet Jeremiah echoed God's warning with these words:

> [The God of Israel says:] "I will be merciful only if you stop your evil thoughts and deeds and start treating each other with justice; only if you stop exploiting foreigners, orphans, and widows." (JEREMIAH 7:5–6)

> "This is what the LORD says: Be fair-minded and just. Do what is right! Help those who have been robbed; rescue them from their oppressors. Quit your evil deeds! Do not mistreat foreigners, orphans, and widows." (JEREMIAH 22:3)

In line with the Old Testament prophets, Jesus also turned racist attitudes upside-down. In the Sermon on the Mount, delivered to a Jewish audience, he said:

> "If a soldier [a Roman] demands that you carry his gear for a mile, carry it two miles. . . . You have heard the law that says, 'Love your neighbor' and hate your enemy. But I say, love your enemies! Pray for those who persecute you! In that way, you will be acting as true children of your Father in heaven." (MATTHEW 5:41, 43–45)

What? Yes, love your enemies and pray for those who persecute you. It was a radical reversal, not only of the normal human tendency, but also of what would have been considered an acceptable response to an enemy and a persecutor.

For centuries, God had repeatedly made his position clear. No Jewish believer in the first century could have claimed ignorance to justify any discrimination against the foreigners, orphans, or widows in their midst. The leaders of the first Christian communities in Jerusalem knew this.

Greek widows in the church needed food just as the Hebrew widows did. Something had to be done about this:

> So the Twelve called a meeting of all the believers. They said, "We apostles should spend our time teaching the word of God, not running a food program. And so, brothers, select seven men who are well respected and are full of the Spirit and wisdom. We will give them this responsibility. Then we apostles can spend our time in prayer and teaching the word."
>
> Everyone liked this idea, and they chose the following: Stephen (a man full of faith and the Holy Spirit), Philip, Procorus, Nicanor, Timon, Parmenas, and Nicolas of Antioch (an earlier convert to the Jewish faith). These seven were presented to the apostles, who prayed for them as they laid their hands on them. (ACTS 6:2–6)

One of the encouraging aspects of this story is how swiftly the apostles addressed the issue when they realized what was going on. And the folks chosen to handle a more equitable food distribution included five men with very Greek names: Procorus, Nicanor, Timon, Parmenas, and Nicholas of Antioch. Stephen and Philip may also have been Greek, but if not, they gave some balance to the work team assembled to address the problem. In any case, discrimination wasn't tolerated. Leaders recognized the issue and took swift steps to rectify it.

WIDOWHOOD IN THE FIRST-CENTURY ROMAN EMPIRE

As you read the story of the Jewish and Greek widows in Acts 5, you might have wondered, "What's the big deal? We can't be talking about very many widows here." But step back and think about what it meant to be a widow in the first century of the Christian era.

As noted in chapter 1, it was common for families (Jewish, Greek, or Roman) to arrange a marriage for a daughter while she was very young, with the wedding taking place soon after the girl began menstruating. So marriage was basically a girl's passage from childhood to adulthood with no adolescence in between. In many cases, young girls married men twice or even three times their age. Conceivably, a young woman could be widowed more than once in her lifetime.

Scholars note that the average life expectancy in the Greco-Roman Empire at that time was roughly twenty-five years for men. Because the Empire was often fighting wars on some front, many men were casualties of battle. Or, if their army unit was defeated in a particular battle, the captured soldiers would be carried off as slaves to the alien conquerors. You can understand why the life expectancy of men could be so low. These realities meant that many women were widowed, often relatively early in life.

Widowhood was so common that marriage laws in the Empire shifted to include something called *sine manu*, meaning "without hand." Earlier, during the Roman Republic, a woman's dowry (the wealth her family provided to her new husband) became the husband's property when she married. But by the first century, if the marriage was established from the beginning as *sine manu*, the woman's dowry remained her own so that in case of either divorce or the death of her husband, she had resources to get on with her life. However, the dowry system worked only for people with sufficient wealth to finance one. Marriage for most couples did not include a dowry. When a woman was widowed, she was often completely without any resources to support herself.

Thus we have stories of widows and their needs in many places in the New Testament. In Luke 7, we read the sad story of a widow following the bier of her only son for burial. She had already lost her husband; now her only other source of support was gone. Jesus intervened and restored her son to life, but for many widows in the first century, there was no miracle.

Think back to the widows in the story of Dorcas. When Peter arrived in Joppa, he found that "the room was filled with widows who were weeping and showing him the coats and other clothes Dorcas had made for them" (Acts 9:39). These women were part of the poor of Joppa who needed very basic items of clothing. Dorcas and her work provided merely one example of the early Christians' response to the widespread need to care for "widows, orphans, and the stranger in the land." Thus, it's not surprising that the early church took up the responsibility to make sure that all of the Christian widows had something to eat every day.

Why would those who doled out the food discriminate against Greek-speaking widows? The answer may have something to do with mutual suspicions between the Jews and their Roman rulers. While the Greek-speaking widows would not be a threat in and of themselves, it's likely that they had been lumped in with the powerful forces of the external Roman rulers. As noted earlier, one of the grand hopes of some of Jesus's disciples early on was that he would raise up an army and throw out Roman rule and its oppressive and cruel practices (such as crucifixion as a means of execution). By betraying Jesus, Judas may actually have been trying to force his hand, thinking that Jesus would not submit to death, but would use his miraculous powers to begin the fight that would end Roman rule over Israel. Roman soldiers stationed in Israel constantly dealt with uprisings against Roman rule. It's not unusual for the ruled to hate their rulers. An extension of that is to hit back any way you can at those who are not your own kind. Jewish believers in the early church would not have been immune to this way of thinking, which may have caused them to feel justified in discriminating against the Greek-speaking widows.

MORE FIRST-CENTURY RACIST CHRISTIANS

If this were the only time in the New Testament in which we are confronted by racism, we might dismiss it as a one-off. But it turns out that racism persisted among believers in other parts of the Roman Empire. More often than we would wish, discussion in the letters of the apostles had to do with the persistent problem of some Christians looking down on other Christians with a different skin color or different ideas or different values. Jews were suspicious of Gentiles and vice versa. The issue of race came up again and again in the first-century churches.

Early in his letter to the church at Rome, the apostle Paul had to address this issue:

> Should we conclude that we Jews are better than others? No, not at all, for we have already shown that all people, whether Jews or Gentiles, are under the power of sin. As the Scriptures say, "No one is righteous—not even one." (ROMANS 3:9–10)

The racism among Roman Christians wasn't as obvious as denying Greek widows their allotment of food. It was more subtle and rested on Jewish Christians' belief in their superior religious knowledge and practices. Because Christianity began within Judaism, Jewish Christians in Rome had to be reminded that *"everyone* has sinned; we *all* fall short of God's glorious standard" (Romans 3:23, emphasis added). There is no room for racism or any form of discrimination in the body of Christ.

The writer of that letter to the Roman Christians was uniquely qualified to write what he did: Paul was a Jew. In fact, he was a Pharisee, trained in the Jewish law under the noted rabbi Gamaliel. So he was an ardent member of the most strictly observant religious group in Israel. At the same time, having been born in Tarsus, a Roman provincial capital, he was a Roman citizen. He had grown up outside Israel in the province of Cilicia. He spoke both Latin and Greek as well as Hebrew or Aramaic. He knew the gentile mind as well as the Jewish law. Perhaps no one else was as qualified as Paul to address the problem of racism among Roman Christians.

In a different letter to the Christians in the province of Galatia, Paul insisted, "There is no longer Jew or Gentile, slave or free, male and female. For you are all one in Christ Jesus" (Galatians 3:28). The human tendency to build hierarchies based on race or class or gender should have no place among followers of Jesus Christ. We are one in Christ. Period.

But that message had to be reiterated over and over among the early Christians. James, the half-brother of Jesus, described the problem this way:

My dear brothers and sisters, how can you claim to have faith in our glorious Lord Jesus Christ if you favor some people over others?

For example, suppose someone comes into your meeting dressed in fancy clothes and expensive jewelry, and another comes in who is poor and dressed in dirty clothes. If you give special attention and a good seat to the rich person, but you say to the poor one, "You can stand over there, or else sit on the floor"—well, doesn't this discrimination show that your judgments are guided by evil motives? . . .

What good is it, dear brothers and sisters, if you say you have faith but don't show it by your actions? Can that kind of faith save anyone? Suppose you see a brother or sister who has no food or clothing, and you say, "Good-bye and have a good day; stay warm and eat well"—but then you don't give that person any food or clothing. What good does that do?

So you see, faith by itself isn't enough. Unless it produces good deeds, it is dead and useless. (JAMES 2:1–4, 14–17)

Here, James uses a negative example to make his positive point: faith is inadequate if we don't pair it with good deeds. In fact, his language is even stronger: Such faith is "dead and useless." Are we tempted to think that the writer is exaggerating the importance of caring for those whose needs we see and we have the means to address? He is not.

OUR CALLING AS FOLLOWERS OF JESUS

Most of us can learn from negative examples. A bad sunburn may teach us the importance of using sunscreen when outdoors in the summer. A low grade on a test may spur us to improve our study habits. Seeing Janie excluded from the boat club building because she was Jewish taught me more about racism than a lecture on the subject. Negative examples can prompt us to rethink situations we might previously have taken for granted. For those of us who call ourselves followers of Jesus Christ, a negative example can confront us with the reality of sin in ways we might otherwise ignore. We need God's Spirit guiding us to reflect on our own attitudes through examples we can understand.

So we study the case of the Greek widows—part of the body of Christ in the new churches being formed—and we listen to James as he reminds us that discrimination can take many forms. In the process, as God's Spirit leads us, we determine not to be party to any kind of hierarchy that puts down one group of people and elevates another. When we refuse to harbor a mind-set that sets one group over another, we reflect the example of Jesus Christ:

> Though he was God, he did not think of equality with God as something to cling to. Instead, he gave up his divine privileges; he took the humble position of a slave and was born as a human being. When he appeared in human form, he humbled himself in obedience to God and died a criminal's death on a cross. (PHILIPPIANS 2:6–8)

In light of that paradigm-shattering example set by Jesus, the apostle Paul tells us, "You must have the same attitude that Christ Jesus had."

As you consider your own biases and what following Jesus's example might mean for you, who is it that first comes to mind? It might be a coworker, or someone you dislike at church, or some prominent person you've seen on television. In what ways might your posture toward that individual fall short of the "same attitude that Christ Jesus had"? In what ways do you sense the Spirit of God might be guiding you to learn from the negative examples of racism and discrimination?

Perhaps it's time to take stock, to reflect on how you really think about and behave toward the folks around you with a different skin color, or a different economic status, or a gender opposite your own. Taking stock can lead you to pray that God's Spirit will help you grasp how your attitude toward others might change if you took Jesus's example seriously. At times, God's Spirit can lead us through negative examples to greater growth and transformation.

• • •

QUESTIONS FOR PERSONAL REFLECTION OR GROUP DISCUSSION

1. As you think back over your own life experience, when were you consciously aware of any kind of discrimination (toward someone else or toward yourself)? Was the discrimination subtle or blatant? How did you respond to it?

2. Sadly, racism and discrimination have persisted for millennia, even within the body of Christ. And while it seems easy to recognize and condemn prejudice in previous generations, it remains much harder to recognize and address in our own. How do you imagine Christians a hundred years from now might assess racism and prejudice in this generation of the Body of Christ—in the church at large as well as in your own Christian community? What subtle or blatant attitudes or practices might they point to as evidence of failing the "attitude Christ had"?

3. In what ways, if any, would you say the Spirit of God has led you by negative example recently? How does the negative example challenge you? What are you learning and how is it changing your thinking or behavior?

4

Lydia
God's Spirit Guides Us through
Spiritual Dissatisfaction

In the industrialized world, anyone who wants to start a new business usually has to raise a huge amount of money, often from venture capitalists. But in the developing world, a loan of a hundred dollars is enough to enable a woman mired in poverty to begin a small business and then to repay the loan. Micro-financing, as it's often called, keeps the funds circulating by passing repaid loans on to another woman, making it possible for her also to begin a business. The loans might be used to buy chickens that enable a woman to sell eggs in the community. Or she may have a skill in basket weaving or jewelry creation and can turn that into a profitable business when she can purchase the tools and supplies of her trade. The businesses are small, but they give women a way to support their families and even pay school fees so their children can be educated. When I have a bit of money set aside to contribute to a charity, often I look for this kind of opportunity to help a woman in another part of the world start her own small business.

Researchers have found that women in the developing world are often more astute and responsible business entrepreneurs than the men in their communities. Because it usually falls to the women to provide food and clothing for their children, they are often much more aware of the daily challenges of meeting even the most minimum needs of their families. So when they are given an opportunity to earn money by creating their own small business, they bring a mother's determination to its success. It turns out that when you or I make a small investment in such a woman, it is not money wasted. The woman receiving that help will succeed because her family's welfare depends on it. Researchers have also found that what may begin as a one-woman operation often develops into a community-wide enterprise. Successful businesswomen often bring other women along as either employees or to franchise their business. In that way an entire town can benefit from one small investment in one determined woman.

Author and leadership consultant Sally Helgesen calls women in business "everyday revolutionaries." Why? The reasons are complex, but in general women create or run businesses with flexible structures that give more opportunities for input to folks throughout the company. There appears to be a distinct female ability to create and lead others in what Helgesen has called "a web of inclusion." This is not the usual top–down kind of leadership. Listening to folks down the chain of command builds a stronger commitment in workers to the success of the business and also increases a leader's understanding of what needs to happen from the ground up. This is a gift that women uniquely bring to today's business world.

Whatever lies behind this female advantage, it's not a recent phenomenon—women have built successful businesses from early times. So it should not surprise us that, when we turn to Acts 16, we meet a successful and influential businesswoman named Lydia. But to put a context around her story, we first need the backstory of someone else, the apostle Paul.

THE APOSTLE PAUL'S BACKSTORY

Recall that Paul was a convert to Christianity who had a unique background: he was a Jew, educated under the noted rabbi Gamaliel. He was also a Pharisee, a member of the strictest Jewish sect in first-century Palestine (Philippians 3:5). But he was born in Tarsus (Acts 22:3), a Roman city with Roman laws, Roman customs, and possibly the Latin language, so he had Roman citizenship. Tarsus, however, was in Cilicia in the southeast corner of Turkey, a part of the Roman Empire with a strong Greek tradition and language. So Paul would have been fluent in Greek, knowledgeable in Roman ways, and a Jew with a deep understanding of the Old Testament Scriptures.

This broad cultural and ethnic background gave Paul a unique ability to serve as one of the first missionaries sent out by the new Christian communities. From his base in present-day Syria (Antioch of Syria, Acts 11:19, 26), he traveled widely, establishing new churches across Asia Minor (now Turkey) and Greece. Each of his three missionary journeys spanned long periods of time, enough to spend weeks, months, or even years in each city. Once settled in a new location, he would preach in the local synagogue, meet with interested folks (both Jews and Gentiles), and eventually establish a church in each town.

Our story picks up when Paul, now on his second missionary journey, has visited the churches in Asia Minor (Turkey) that had been started on his previous missionary trip. At one of those churches, the Christian congregation at Lystra, he invited a young man named Timothy to join him. Timothy's mother, Eunice (2 Timothy 1:5), was ethnically Jewish and religiously a follower of Jesus Christ. Timothy's father was a Gentile, ethnically Greek. Paul didn't know it at the time, but God's Spirit was about to move him from Turkey to Greece for the first time. The Greek culture might present subtle but important cultural differences for a first-time traveler there and an ethnically Greek companion traveling with him could be important to the team in the days ahead.

Paul, Silas, and Timothy were heading toward a new Turkish territory called Bithynia, but "the Spirit of Jesus did not allow them to go there. So instead, they went on through Mysia, to the seaport of Troas" (on Turkey's northwest coast) (Acts 16:7–8). That night, "Paul had a vision: A man from Macedonia in northern Greece was standing there, pleading with him, 'Come over to Macedonia and help us!'" (Acts 16:9). Immediately, the trio set sail from Troas across the northern tip of the Aegean sea to Neapolis. This was the seaport for Philippi, "a major city of the district of Macedonia and a Roman colony" (Acts 16:12). God's Spirit had directed this trio to leave Turkey and head to Greece, specifically to the city of Philippi in the region of Macedonia.

Philippi was near a major battleground where, in 42

BC, Antony and Octavian had defeated the partisans of the Republic. The victors then released some of their veteran soldiers into the city, giving them each a square of land and pronouncing the town a Roman colony. So Philippi became a "miniature Rome" under Roman law, governed by two military officers appointed directly by Rome. Paul's Roman citizenship would turn out to be vitally important in Philippi.

Up to this point, Paul and his companions, upon entering a new city, usually headed to the Jewish synagogue where they could engage Jews in conversation about Jesus. But Philippi had no synagogue, possibly because a synagogue required a minimum of ten Jewish males before it could be organized. The city may have lacked that many Jewish males.

It was the Sabbath. A Jewish holy day would mean nothing to folks in a Roman colony, but for the apostle Paul and his companions observing the Jewish Sabbath was important. Without a local synagogue in which to worship, they would have to look for some God-worshipers elsewhere. So where was he to start? The text tells us Paul's alternative:

> On the Sabbath we went a little way outside the city to a riverbank, where we thought people would be meeting for prayer, and we sat down to speak with some women who had gathered there. One of them was Lydia from Thyatira, a merchant of expensive purple cloth, who worshiped God. (Acts 16:13–14)

Whatever else Paul might have expected to find that morning, God's Spirit led him straight to a woman with a heart open to God.

A Prosperous Businesswoman Becomes the First Convert in Greece

"Lydia from Thyatira, a merchant of expensive purple cloth, who worshiped God." In that one sentence, we learn three important things about this woman. The first is that she is from the Turkish city of Thyatira, not a Greek city, but a city in northern Asia Minor. So Lydia is not a local born and bred. She has moved to Philippi from a different land.

The second thing we learn about Lydia is that she is "a merchant of expensive purple cloth." What was that about? Thyatira was internationally known for its trade guilds. One of the most powerful guilds in Thyatira was the group of merchants making purple dye and weaving cloth from the dyed yarns. Lydia was one of the guild sellers of purple-dyed clothing. Purple dye was very expensive, and to be part of that guild in Thyatira meant that Lydia was a person of means, probably very wealthy. It's likely that she employed others to carry out the dyeing and weaving of the garments she sold. We know from the biblical text that she was a successful businesswoman.

The third thing the text tells us about this woman is that she "worshiped God." While that may not initially seem significant to us, in the first-century Roman world, worship of anyone but the emperor was dangerous. In a Roman city like Philippi, the Imperial Cult (the worship of the emperor) dominated religious observance. Scholar Rick Wade has noted:

> In the days of the Roman empire, the worship of pagan gods and the emperor was a part of everyone's life. . . .

Christians' reluctance to offer worship to the emperor and the gods was considered madness, considering what would happen to them if they didn't. Why not just offer a pinch of incense to the image of the emperor?[1]

That would be true across the Empire but it was particularly important in a Roman city like Philippi. Though the text tells us that Lydia worshiped God (a "God-fearer" in some translations), she may nevertheless have had few qualms about following the custom of offering a pinch of incense to the emperor once a year.

WHO OR WHAT WAS A "GOD-FEARER"?

Men and women who worshiped God were usually called "God-fearers." What did that mean? New Testament scholar Lynn Cohick tells us that "God-fearers were gentile women and men who stood on the boundary between Judaism and paganism and often Christianity as well. They were attracted but had not become proselytes."[2] Lydia, a Gentile, was one who stood on that boundary between Judaism and paganism, open to truth but unsure where to find it. She was what we might refer to today as a "seeker."

The Greek and Roman worlds were populated with numerous gods based on human traits that essentially determined their actions. For example, Aphrodite (the Roman goddess Venus) was the goddess of love, beauty, and desire. She was married to Hephaestus, the god of fire and the forge, but she had many adulterous affairs. Hermes (the Roman god Mercury) was the messenger of the gods. Zeus (the Roman god Jupiter) was king of the gods, but was the youngest child of two Titans. Most of the Greek and Roman gods and goddesses were nevertheless very "human" in their weaknesses and foibles.

Centuries earlier, the Greek poet Homer had captured much of the Greek pantheon of gods in his epic work *The Iliad*. The Roman mythology, including its own list of gods and goddesses, was later explored in the *Aeneid*. But pantheons of gods go back much earlier in history, and in the Old Testament we learn about local Canaanite gods who were each responsible for success in some limited area. For example, one god would be responsible for rain, another for bountiful crops, still another for fertility in animals or in human families. In similar fashion, different Greek gods were popular in different towns for different reasons. We see reverence for the goddess Diana (also called Artemis) in Ephesus, and in Corinth the greatest of all the temples there venerated the goddess Aphrodite.

We might shake our heads and wonder how first-century people could be so gullible. But before we write them off, we may want to think about the ways in which we place our allegiance and trust in things other than the one true God. Although we may not bow down to a statue made of marble or wood, we can still find ourselves in service of a long list of gods—the god of money, the god of popularity, the god of security, the god of sports, the god of fine dining, the god of fashion, the god of beauty, and on and on. Just because we don't have stone images on a shelf in our homes where we offer a pinch of incense several times each day doesn't mean we are innocent of idolatry. Whatever (or whomever) we might "idolize" becomes an idol for us. Whatever might receive an inordinate amount of our time or resources may be an idol for us. Our credit card bills may nudge us to an awareness of a god we didn't even realize we worship. While we may go to church each Sunday, we might discover that the God of the Bible has gotten lost in our worship of other gods.

But across the Roman Empire in the first century were men and women like Lydia who didn't buy into the gods popular in their communities. These were folks who had already turned away intellectually from worship of the local and national gods of their town or province. They were open to the possibility of an alternative. But what? Though they didn't know it, God's Spirit was leading them to question these local deities and to consider the Jewish idea of a single, all-powerful God.

What little they knew about the Hebrew God led them to fear him. The Old Testament picture of a single God who was all-knowing, everywhere-present, and all-powerful inspired awe and fear. For that reason they were called God-fearers. For the most part, they were sympathetic to Judaism and would listen to anyone who preached in a local Jewish synagogue. As the apostles preached across the Roman Empire, these God-fearers were seeking truth and were ready to give attention to what they were being told.

Inscriptions on everything from vases to buildings tell us that up to 80 percent of the God-fearers in the Roman Empire were women. For this reason, they represent an important part of the Christian congregations being formed. Though they didn't count in the formation of Jewish synagogues—which tallied only the men in determining the size of any congregation—they became vital to the birth and life of the new Christian churches. That most of the God-fearers in the first century were women may surprise us. And yet it was they who were most likely to question and reject the panoply of gods and goddesses being worshiped in their communities. As a result, God's Spirit used them to influence others to give the gospel a hearing.

These God-fearing women were often in audiences that the apostles encountered as they preached across the Roman Empire. They were determined seekers who wanted to know more. And so we find the God-fearing Gentile Lydia among the women gathered that Sabbath at the river for prayer, led there by God's Spirit. Luke describes what happened next:

> As she listened to us, the Lord opened her heart, and she accepted what Paul was saying. She and her household were baptized, and she asked us to be her guests. "If you agree that I am a true believer in the Lord," she said, "come and stay at my home." And she urged us until we agreed. (ACTS 16:14–15)

We know Lydia as Paul's first convert to Christianity in Greece. Beyond that and her occupation, we know little else about her. The text mentions no husband, so most scholars assume she was a widow. But it's also possible that she was married and her husband was away for long periods of time on business. It is clear that she was the person in charge of her home, leading other members of her household to join her in embracing faith in Jesus Christ and acknowledging that publicly through baptism. Also, she was the one who invited Paul and Silas to stay in her house as her guests. Scholars tell us that Paul and his two companions stayed in her home in Philippi for close to three months, teaching the new Christians and establishing a congregation that met in this successful businesswoman's house.

PERILS, PROGRESS, AND PROMINENT PEOPLE IN FIRST-CENTURY EVANGELISM

Paul's missionary journey to Philippi was fruitful, but it was not without perils. One day, Paul and Silas had an encounter with evil men who received income derived from the antics of a demon-possessed girl. When Paul cast out the demon and the girl lost her fortune-telling powers, her handlers instigated a riot. Paul and Silas were arrested, severely beaten, and then thrown in jail. You may know the story of the earthquake in the middle of the night that flung open prison doors and released all of the prisoners from their shackles. But the apostles did not flee when they had the opportunity, which would have brought a death sentence for the officer in charge. In gratitude, the jailer brought the two apostles to his house, fed them, cared for their wounds, and listened to their message. God's Spirit opened his heart, and he and his entire household believed in Jesus as Savior and were immediately baptized (Acts 16:16–34).

As Roman citizens from birth, Paul and Silas should never have been beaten and jailed without a trial. When the city fathers realized what they had allowed to happen, they tried to get Paul and his companions to leave town quietly. But because the beating had been public, Paul insisted on a public show of penitence:

Paul replied, "They have publicly beaten us without a trial and put us in prison—and we are Roman citizens. So now they want us to leave secretly? Certainly not! Let them come themselves to release us!"

When the police reported this, the city officials were alarmed to learn that Paul and Silas were Roman citizens. So they came to the jail and apologized to them. Then they brought them out and begged them to leave the city. When Paul and Silas left the prison, they returned to the home of Lydia. There they met with the believers and encouraged them once more. Then they left town. (ACTS 16:37–40)

Note that Paul and his companions didn't hurry to leave Philippi. They had a band of new believers in Jesus Christ who needed further encouragement. Despite the urging of city officials, the apostles stayed long enough to insure that these new followers of Jesus had enough knowledge to flourish in their faith.

But also note where Paul and his companions went next— to Thessalonica (Acts 17:1). The distance from Philippi to Thessalonica was 171 kilometers, roughly 100 miles. Today, the Egnatian E90 limited-access highway allows motorists to cover that distance in less than two hours, but in the first-century Roman Empire, the rough, cobbled road was most often covered on foot. Have you ever tried walking 100 miles to get from one point to another? How long would that take you? What kind of commitment would compel you to walk that distance to the next potential ministry site? With no fast-food restaurants or comfortable motels along the route, the apostles' travel was time-consuming and any-thing but easy.

That long hike from Philippi eventually brought Paul, Silas, and Timothy to Thessalonica, where there was a Jewish synagogue.

> As was Paul's custom, he went to the synagogue service, and for three Sabbaths in a row he used the Scriptures to reason with the people. He explained the prophecies and proved that the Messiah must suffer and rise from the dead. . . . Some of the Jews who listened were persuaded and joined Paul and Silas, along with many God-fearing Greek men *and quite a few prominent women.* (ACTS 17:2–4, emphasis added)

Did you note who was listening to Paul on those three Sabbaths? Not just Jews listened to him. Greek God-fearing men and quite a few prominent women were in his audience.

Once again, God's Spirit was present and opened hearts to the Good News of God's love for all nations. Gentiles as well as Jews could be forgiven and made part of the family of faith. But while some embraced the gospel message, other Jews in Thessalonica were incensed by it.

> Some of the Jews were jealous, so they gathered some troublemakers from the marketplace to form a mob and start a riot . . . [telling the city council that] "Paul and Silas have caused trouble all over the world, . . . and now they are here disturbing our city, too. And Jason has welcomed them into his home. They are all guilty of treason against Caesar, for they profess allegiance to another king, named Jesus." (ACTS 17:5–7)

Not surprisingly, that same night the new believers in Thessalonica sent Paul and Silas on to Berea, another long hike of forty-five miles or seventy-two kilometers. Once again, they first went to the Jewish synagogue.

> The people of Berea were more open-minded than those in Thessalonica, and they listened eagerly to Paul's message. They searched the Scriptures day after day to see if Paul and Silas were teaching the truth. As a result, many Jews believed, *as did many of the prominent Greek women* and men. (ACTS 17:11–12, emphasis added)

Are you seeing the pattern here? Across northern Greece in major cities, God's Spirit has reached into the hearts of many prominent Greek women and men.

PROMINENT WOMEN

Who were these prominent women who became believers in Jesus Christ? In chapter 1, we met Mary Magdalene, Joanna, Susanna, and other women who could travel openly in Jesus's band in a culture that routinely sequestered women. We learned that because they were benefactors supplying the basic physical needs of Jesus and the twelve disciples, they had a visibility and acceptance not granted to other women. In similar fashion, as Paul and his companions crisscrossed the Roman Empire on the north side of the Mediterranean Sea, they frequently found acceptance of their message by prominent women, including businesswomen like Lydia. Why might Luke be at pains to note the presence of these women in describing Paul's journeys to town after town in Greece?

God's Spirit was clearly at work in these women's lives in ways that would benefit the newly formed congregations of Jesus-followers. These women were prominent—they had acceptance and influence in their communities. People esteemed and listened to them because of their integrity and community standing. In spite of the centuries-long influence of philosophers Plato and Aristotle (who taught that women were gullible, promiscuous, and in every way inferior to men), statues of prominent women had been erected in numerous Greek cities to honor many of them.

What would it take to be known as a prominent woman? Most likely, these women were affluent, educated, and socially well-connected. Like Mary Magdalene, Joanna, Susanna, and the other women of Luke 8, some of them may have been benefactors, using their wealth to aid others. Others may have been successful businesswomen like Lydia. Some may have been widows. In all likelihood, their prominence didn't rest entirely on being married to men of means but came from their own involvement in the community. When they showed an interest in the gospel, this might have created interest in others to consider the Good News that Paul and his companions preached.

As people of influence and means, they likely also had homes large enough to serve as meeting places for believers. Throughout the New Testament letters we find church after church being started and maintained in homes belonging to women (Acts 16:40, Romans 16:3–5, 1 Corinthians 1:11, Colossians 4:15). They understood that what they possessed had come from God's hand, and they used what God had given them to benefit the growing churches. We see that in Lydia, the riverside God-fearer who, in response to Paul's message, immediately shared the Good News with her entire household. That household could have included workers in her business as well as servants maintaining her property. With her, they were all baptized, and it was in Lydia's house that the first church was born and nurtured on Greek soil. Lydia used all that God had given her to advance the truth she had embraced and wanted shared with others.

Using Our Influence for God's Purposes

Influence is the effect or power that one person has to change how another person thinks or acts. We all have influence. But that influence can be good or bad, depending on how we choose to use it. Do we choose to model honesty, or are we careless about telling the truth? Do we choose to model generosity or are we stingy? People who admire us may follow whatever example we set. So how we use our influence can have either a positive or negative impact on impressionable children or friends or others.

Lydia had influence. She had wealth, a large house, and contacts in both Thyatira and Philippi. We're encouraged when we see how she used the influence God had given her. She immediately shared her newfound faith in Jesus Christ with everyone in her household. She then opened her large home to the apostles and to all who joined her in learning about the Christian life. Lydia models influence well used for good purposes.

Note how God's Spirit was at work, first leading Paul and his companions to leave Turkey and cross over into Greece, then leading them to the most influential woman who was open to the message of Jesus Christ. At the same time, God's Spirit had already been at work in Lydia's life, enabling her to turn away from the gods and goddesses of her community to embrace the one true God. Now, as Paul and his companions walked the river's shore, God's Spirit led them to Lydia.

God's Spirit still works to lead and guide us in similar ways today. The apostle Paul noted this in his letter to the Romans, when he reminded them, "God causes everything to work together for the good of those who love God" (Romans 8:28). That is God's Spirit at work, leading us even when we might not recognize his presence in our life.

• • •

QUESTIONS FOR PERSONAL REFLECTION OR GROUP DISCUSSION

1. Aside from your parents or childhood caregivers, who would you say has had the greatest positive influence on you? In what ways has that person's influence shaped you?

2. What kinds of things did your spiritual influencers say or do that affected you?

3. Who would you say has influenced your spiritual thinking most recently? Share the reasons for your response.

4. Who first comes to mind when you think about those within your circle of influence? If you could have a positive influence on them in some way within the next twenty-four hours, what would you like it to be? Why?

5

Damaris
God's Spirit Guides Us to Truth
in a False Culture

Most of us live in cultures in which spinning the truth, if not outright lying, seems to be okay. We take for granted that politicians will promise anything—no matter how outlandish—to get our vote. We're not surprised to hear news reports of yet another manufacturer caught in a web of deceptive claims about some product. And far from being the exception, corruption in local and national civic institutions seems to be the rule. We may grumble about this state of affairs from time to time, but in the end we just take them as examples of a culture in which some form of deception is simply "business as usual."

One of the challenges of living in such a culture is that if the lies are repeated often enough and believed by enough people, we can easily fall victim to widespread deception: we believe something that isn't true simply because most of the folks around us believe that it *is* true. At that point, our culture goes beyond telling us what to believe and actually blinds us to truthful alternatives. Historian Anne Firor Scott warns us about this:

> It is a truism, yet one easy to forget, that people see most easily things they are prepared to see and overlook those they do not expect to encounter. . . . Because our minds are clouded, we do not see things that are before our eyes. What clouds our minds is, of course, the culture that at any time teaches us what to see and what not to see.[1]

It's not always easy to resist the lies whispered to us by the culture all day long. But in the end, how we respond to those lies really matters. What we believe to be true about our purpose in life or about God makes all the difference in how we live our lives every day. It's not just a one-off. It's a lifelong way of thinking and living. So it's important that we know the truth—about God, about ourselves, and about this world and the world to come.

This isn't a new problem for us in the twenty-first century. Discerning truth from error has challenged thinking people almost from the beginning of time. A woman named Damaris in ancient Athens struggled with it as she evaluated the spin put on truth by the major thinkers of her day. Were any of them telling the truth? How could she know what was really true?

Even then the problem of discerning truth was not new. In the Old Testament, Job's friends spun their version of the truth even as suffering Job clung to what he was sure was true. In the end, God vindicated Job, condemning his friends for their corruption of the truth.

When we turn to the New Testament, we find Jesus going head-to-head with religious leaders who were spinning God's truth in false ways. His closest followers struggled to understand what they should believe about God and a person's relationship to that God. In the middle of Jesus's trumped-up trial, even the Roman governor Pilate raised the question of truth. Listen in on this snippet of conversation between him and Jesus:

> Then Pilate . . . called for Jesus to be brought to him. "Are you the king of the Jews?" he asked him.
>
> Jesus replied, "Is this your own question or did others tell you about me?"
>
> "Am I a Jew?" Pilate retorted. "Your own people and their leading priests brought you to me for trial. Why? What have you done?"
>
> Jesus answered, "My Kingdom is not an earthly kingdom. If it were, my followers would fight to keep me from being handed over to the Jewish leaders. But my Kingdom is not of this world."
>
> Pilate said, "So you are a king?"
>
> Jesus responded, "You say I am a king. Actually, I was born and came into the world to testify to the truth. All who love the truth recognize that what I say is true."
>
> "What is truth?" Pilate asked. (JOHN 18:33–38)

We don't know the tone of voice in which Pilate asked that last question. Was he being sarcastic? Bitter? Serious?

Jesus came into the world to "testify to the truth"—to reveal the truth about God to people steeped in falsehoods. Pilate knew that Jesus was innocent of the charges the Jewish leaders were making. Yet he was caught between their repeated and pervasive falsehoods and the truth about Jesus and his mission.

Thinking people had long been haunted by Pilate's question—*What is truth?* Four hundred years earlier, the brilliant Greek philosopher Plato made it a central question in his reflections. At one point he asked, "Isn't it a bad thing to be deceived about the truth and a good thing to know what the truth is? For I assumed that by knowing the truth you mean knowing things as they really are." Another time he asked, "Is there anything more closely connected with wisdom than truth?"

Plato's questions so resonated with Greek culture and thought that for centuries those who came after him continued to wrestle with what was true. By the time the apostle Paul arrived in Greece, public discourse about truth had become a national pastime. In our last chapter, we met the God-fearer Lydia whose search for "things as they really are" ended in truth found at a riverside prayer meeting with the apostle Paul in Philippi. Now we meet an intellectual woman named Damaris listening to every kind of Athenian teacher, also searching for truth in the midst of a million falsehoods. What were some of her options?

THE "LATEST IDEAS" ABOUT TRUTH IN ATHENS

When the apostle Paul's missionary journey took him from Berea to Athens, he entered a city and a culture steeped in falsehoods about God. Everywhere he turned, he found idols. Luke picks up the story in these words:

> While Paul was waiting [for Silas and Timothy] in Athens, he was deeply troubled by all the idols he saw everywhere in the city. He went to the synagogue to reason with the

Jews and the God-fearing Gentiles, and spoke daily in the public square to all who happened to be there.

He also had a debate with some of the Epicurean and Stoic philosophers. (Acts 17:16–18)

Did you catch how many different groups of people Paul engaged in debate about the gospel? Jews, God-fearing Gentiles, Epicurean and Stoic philosophers. Think about the breadth of knowledge he brought to those four very differ ent audiences. In the synagogue, likely speaking in Hebrew, he could reason with the Jews only because he could draw upon a deep knowledge of God's dealings with the Hebrew nation and the promise of a Messiah, whom God had now sent into the world. In the synagogues, he also interacted with the Gentile God-fearers present, using the Old Testament Scriptures with them in ways that drew them to faith in the God-man, Jesus Christ. But not only did Paul spend time in the synagogue; he was also out in the public square talking with anyone who was interested, and he engaged in debates with both the Epicurean and Stoic philosophers.

Let's take a closer look at the Epicureans. Who were they? What did Paul need to know in order to engage in serious discussion with them? Epicureans were followers of the philosopher Epicurus (307 BC), a materialist who attacked all ideas of divine intervention. For materialists, nothing exists except what we can touch or see. There is no God in heaven or anywhere else. Paul would have to know this about them because his message was precisely about the God who is "the King of all kings and Lord of all lords. He alone can never die, and he lives in light so brilliant that no human can approach him. No human eye has ever seen him, nor ever will" (1 Timothy 6:15–16). How do you present the supernatural God to materialists who deny the existence of anything but solid matter? Paul had to find a way to tailor his message about the eternal God to that Epicurean crowd.

If only matter exists, then the highest good on earth would be pleasure. That's why when we hear the word "epicurean" today, we tend to think of people whose life philosophy is some version of "eat, drink, and be merry, for tomorrow we die." Today's Epicureans are devoted to pleasure, to comfort, or to high living because, in their view, that's all there is.

But that wasn't quite what the philosopher Epicurus had in mind. He believed that human beings attain the highest pleasure not from excessive self-indulgence but from living modestly and limiting our desires. If we'd do that, he reasoned, we would become tranquil, and tranquility constitutes the highest form of pleasure or happiness. And there is truth in that. But in Epicurean philosophy, the basis for it lies in denying any supernatural reality, be it Jewish, Christian, or Athenian beliefs about a nonmaterial world.

When the apostle Paul debated the Epicureans, his challenge was to persuade them that a nonmaterial world not only existed, but that it mattered immensely because it was the realm of the eternal, invisible God. At the same time, he had to make clear that the one true God was different from the gods and goddesses in the various Greek religions.

And then there were the Stoics. Who were they? They took their name from the *stoa*, or porch, in the *Agora* (marketplace) where they regularly met. As philosophers, they were relative newcomers, but their central tenets had deep roots in Greek thought.

You may be familiar with the word "stoic" that comes from this ancient Greek philosophical group. It means being able to bear pain or trouble without showing emotions and without complaint. That's a fairly accurate description of the Stoics' basic philosophy. For them, showing emotions, especially emotions of fear or envy or a passionate love for anything, marked a person as a slave to whatever produced that emotion. A wise person was in complete control of his or her emotions, evidenced in patience or resignation. Aristotle had argued that men differed from women in their ability to be "self-contained, firmly bounded." That is to say, men were able to control their emotions in ways that women could not. This, for a Stoic, was considered to be the highest good.

In debating the Stoics, Paul's challenge included presenting to them a God who so loved the world that he invaded it in order to redeem it. We Christians sing, "Love so amazing, so divine, demands my soul, my life, my all." Such a lavish display of love would have been the antithesis of the emotional control a wise Stoic considered essential.

So it's not surprising when we read that Paul's listeners were skeptical when he told them about Jesus and his resurrection:

> They said, "What's this babbler trying to say with these strange ideas he's picked up?" Others said, "He seems to be preaching about some foreign gods."
>
> Then they took him to the high council of the city. "Come and tell us about this new teaching," they said. "You are saying some rather strange things, and we want to know what it's all about." (Acts 17:18–20)

It's likely that Damaris had heard all of these arguments, both Epicurean and Stoic. Given her position in the community, she would have to know the ins and outs of every reason given by these debaters. Otherwise, she would not have been present at this exceptional meeting of the high council.

The "high council" Luke refers to was called the Areopagus (named for their meeting place on the Ares Hill). It was the governing body in Athens at the time. Not long after his arrival, Paul, a newcomer and stranger, was invited to speak to this important group of leaders. This was nothing short of God at work, opening doors Paul was uniquely equipped to enter.

At this point, Luke interrupts his story to remind his readers that, "all the Athenians as well as the foreigners in Athens seemed to spend all their time discussing the latest ideas" (Acts 17:21). It seems that this was a city in which everyone was asking that age-old question, *What is truth?* Luke then gives us the substance of Paul's address to this highly educated audience. Note how cleverly Paul connects to their practices, yet how he weaves in an introduction to God's truth:

> "Men of Athens, I notice that you are very religious in every way, for as I was walking along I saw your many shrines. And one of your altars had this inscription on it: 'To an unknown God.' This God, whom you worship without knowing, is the one I'm telling you about.
>
> "He is the God who made the world and everything in it. Since he is Lord of heaven and earth, he doesn't live in man-made temples, and human hands can't serve his needs—for he has no needs. He himself gives life and

breath to everything, and he satisfies every need. From one man he created all the nations throughout the whole earth. He decided beforehand when they should rise and fall, and he determined their boundaries.

"His purpose was for the nations to seek after God and perhaps feel their way toward him and find him—though he is not far from any one of us. For in him we live and move and exist. As some of your own poets have said, 'We are his offspring.' And since this is true, we shouldn't think of God as an idol designed by craftsmen from gold or silver or stone.

"God overlooked people's ignorance about these things in earlier times, but now he commands everyone everywhere to repent of their sins and turn to him. For he has set a day for judging the world with justice by the man he has appointed, and he proved to everyone who this is by raising him from the dead." (ACTS 17:22–31)

It appears that Paul had their attention until he said, "God proved this by raising Jesus from the dead." At that point, the audience erupted. Some laughed in contempt, but others said that they wanted to hear more at a later time.

Did anything really come from Paul's encounter with that august audience? Well, yes. "Some joined him and became believers. Among them were Dionysius, a member of the council, a woman named Damaris, and others with them" (Acts 17:34).

As noted previously, whenever we see a person's name in Acts or in the apostles' letters, it means that the person was already well known among the churches for his or her ministry. Not all of the new believers were named, but it's clear that both Dionysius and Damaris were singled out among the converts that day for their later, wholehearted, and long-term engagement in ministry.

The conversions of Dionysius and Damaris are a reminder that in the other Greek cities Paul had already visited, many "God-fearing Greek men and quite a few prominent women" became believers in Jesus Christ. In most cases, these new converts were people of influence. Their conversions provided the foundation for new churches wherever the apostles went.

A Woman Intellectual in Athens?

So what was "a woman named Damaris" doing at that meeting of the highest governing body of Athens? Why would she not only be permitted to attend, but also be interested in the philosophical discussions among Athens' elites?

Centuries earlier, the Greek philosopher Aristotle had taught that women would bring disorder and evil to governing. He considered them "utterly useless" and felt they "caused more confusion than the enemy."[2] For this reason, he believed that it was best to keep women separate from the rest of civil society. So for centuries, Athenian married women were sequestered at home with little exposure to the outside world. That's why the presence of Damaris at that exclusive Areopagus meeting where Paul preached is especially intriguing.

Scholars tell us that if a woman was allowed to attend an intellectual debate in a public arena, she was likely to be a *hetaera*, a courtesan (a high-class prostitute). She would be intelligent, well-educated, and able to engage guests intellectually. In many cases, *hetairae* were in long-term relationships with rich and powerful men. We're told that such women were often among the most independent, wealthy, and influential people in Athens.

The Bible doesn't tell us that Damaris was a courtesan, but the fact that she was present—not only in the public square but later at the closed meeting of the Areopagus high council—indicates that she likely was in a relationship with one of Athens' leading men. Furthermore, only a highly educated individual would have been able to follow the philosophical debates that led up to Paul's meeting with the city's leaders on the Ares Hill. What we do know about Damaris from the Bible was that she immediately and wholeheartedly responded to Paul's words and became a follower of Jesus Christ (Acts 17:34). She had enough knowledge of the philosophical and religious alternatives to recognize truth when she heard it.

Because we know her name, we also know that she became a recognized worker in the churches and would have been widely respected. What might someone like Damaris bring to the new churches? Think about one of the basic attributes of a successful *hetaera* in Athens. She was sufficiently skilled in Greek philosophy and debate that she could not only follow a high-level discussion, but also hold her own with the greatest minds in the city. This is a woman different from the businesswoman Lydia or the influential women of Thessalonica and Berea.

Instead of economic and business acumen, it was likely Damaris's keen intellect and ability to interact with educated Athenians that God used for Kingdom impact. She could build theological and philosophical bridges to Athens' elites. Once she became a devout and astute follower of Jesus Christ, she could communicate deep truths about God and salvation with people seeking an alternative to the gods and goddesses of Athenian religion.

In Galilee, God had used wealthy women to support Jesus and his band during his ministry there. In Joppa, God used Dorcas to come to the aid of some of the community's least and lowest, the widows and the poor. In Philippi, God used the businesswoman Lydia to reach others in that Roman city. In Athens, the great intellectual center in the ancient world, God used Damaris—a woman uniquely gifted to become an effective communicator for Jesus Christ and his Kingdom among the intellectual elites of her city.

FINDING THE TRUTH

As we can see in the response to the gospel that Paul encountered all over Greece—in Philippi, in Thessalonica, in Berea, now in Athens—it appears that many prominent men and women were asking Pilate's question deep in their souls: *What is truth? How can we know what is true and what is false?*

It's possible that this hunger for truth was in the Greeks' DNA. Much earlier, their philosopher Plato had written, "What is at issue is the conversion of the mind from the twilight of error to the truth." Somehow, for him, knowing the truth would reveal eternal reality—what really matters in the long run.

Jesus's answer to Pilate is the answer we need to hear today: "My Kingdom is not an earthly kingdom. If it were, my followers would fight to keep me from being handed over to the Jewish leaders. But my Kingdom is not of this world. . . . I was born and came into the world to testify to the truth. All who love the truth recognize that what I say is true" (John 18:36–37).

Not only did Jesus speak truth (revealing God to us human beings), but he assured us of an infallible guide to truth: the Holy Spirit. "The Holy Spirit . . . will teach you everything and will remind you of everything I have told you. I am leaving you with a gift—peace of mind and heart" (John 14:26–27). In fact, just before his arrest, he told his followers, "It is best for you that I go away, because if I don't, the Advocate won't come. If I do go away, then I will send him to you. . . . When the Spirit of truth comes, he will guide you into all truth" (John 16:7, 13).

We know when we resonate with something. Often this is God's Spirit at work, guiding us into truth (John 14:17). God sent Jesus into the world as the Way, the *Truth*, and the Life. Then he gave us the Holy Spirit to lead us into all truth, to guide us in sorting through the myriad false gods, idols, and values that litter our twenty-first century landscape. God's Spirit was present in Athens that day, guiding Damaris to recognize God's truth in a culture rife with error. And God's Spirit is present with us today, enabling us to recognize the truth about Jesus Christ that will support our faith in any culture that thrives on lies and deception.

CAN A HIGH-CLASS PROSTITUTE BECOME A RELIABLE WITNESS IN THE CHURCHES?

Imagine if Damaris's story had taken place not thousands of years ago and thousands of miles away but recently and in your community. How do you imagine you or others might respond if you heard that she was now active in ministry? Chances are that while some would support her, others would question her or perhaps outright condemn her. They might say, "You're telling me that a high-class prostitute is becoming well-known for her ministry in Christian churches? What is wrong with the leaders who let that happen? Look at the kind of person she was. How can we trust anything she says?"

The apostle Paul ran into this kind of judgment again and again. In fact, he had to challenge Jews who said similar things about immoral Gentiles:

> You may think you can condemn such people, but you are just as bad, and you have no excuse! When you say they are wicked and should be punished, you are condemning yourself, for you who judge others do these very same things. . . . Why do you think you can avoid God's judgment when you do the same things? Don't you see how wonderfully kind, tolerant, and patient God is with you? Does this mean nothing to you? (ROMANS 2:1, 3–4)

Later, Paul concluded, "For everyone has sinned; we all fall short of God's glorious standard. Yet God, in his grace, freely makes us right in his sight" (Romans 3:23–24). That's God's final word on a judging spirit. Grace is greater than all our sin. When a woman like Damaris testifies to God's grace in her life, we listen because she is speaking the truth.

Damaris and the city council member Dionysius listened to God's Spirit and made the life-changing decision to become followers of Jesus Christ. Without that decision, their names would have been lost in history's dust. But we honor them today by name because they chose to follow

Jesus Christ and are numbered among those whom God used notably in ministry. They turned from what was false and embraced truth, the truth about God in Christ. God's Spirit led them to the Truth.

I resonate with Damaris. Her prior experience with the many faces of falsehood cleared a path to truth for her. When she heard Paul's message, she could step into its truth. God's Spirit enabled her to become a follower of Jesus Christ and an active participant in the first-century churches. Though I grew up in Christian circles, as a teenager I constantly asked questions deep in my soul about the truth of the Bible's teachings about Jesus and salvation. But as I contemplated the alternatives, I recall one day on my knees telling God that I would live my life "as if what I know about Jesus is true." I wasn't sure, but I had enough to go on that I could trust God for the rest. It was much later in life that I realized that such a decision was the essence of faith—trusting what was unseen but ultimately true.

God's Spirit whispers truth that we can trust, even when we wonder about it. And by God's grace, we live into that truth by faith, discovering one day that it truly is true.

• • •

QUESTIONS FOR PERSONAL REFLECTION OR GROUP DISCUSSION

1. In Athens, Paul encountered diverse philosophies and schools of thought, each with its own ideas about what was most important in life. For example, the Epicureans defined pleasure as tranquility and denied supernatural reality; the Stoics esteemed emotional restraint. If contemporary culture were a formal school of thought, how would you describe what it exalts, esteems, and denies? What messages does it convey about what is most important in life? About what truth is?

2. Damaris was an educated woman with a keen mind. Despite the fact that she lived in a culture immersed in false gods, she recognized and was captivated by Paul's teaching about the one true God. As you reflect on Paul's speech to the Areopagus (Acts 17:22–31), which of his statements do you imagine might have stood out most to Damaris? Why?

3. Over the course of your life, how would you characterize your pursuit of the age-old question, *What is truth?* In what season(s) have you pursued this question most intensely? To what degree is it a question you are pursuing in this season of life? For example, do you think about it and wrestle with it a lot, not at all, somewhere between? Share the reasons for your response.

6

Priscilla and Aquila
God's Spirit Guides Us in Stressful Events

My first exposure to what it meant to be a refugee—someone who has been forced to flee one's country—came through my high school friendship with Monica. Much like the Von Trapp family from *The Sound of Music*, Monica's family had a harrowing escape from Vienna when Nazi forces invaded Austria in March 1938. Her parents, psychoanalysts working closely with Sigmund Freud in the 1930s, knew they had to escape to Switzerland while it was still possible. Their journey by train across Austria was tense as the German Gestapo went up and down the train cars, looking for people like her parents who could be useful to the Third Reich. Once safely in Switzerland, they eventually emigrated to the United States.

It's hard to imagine all of the changes and losses her family experienced as they packed a few bags and left everything else behind in the middle of the night to escape. In addition to losing home and property as well as important family and work relationships, they lost the stability of a familiar neighborhood, knowledge of the community, and the ability to navigate the routines of life with ease. Then they had to take on a host of new challenges—learning English, deciphering different cultural expectations, and navigating prejudice and suspicion that they were somehow aligned with the regime they had risked their lives to escape. It was an extremely stressful and life-defining experience for Monica and her family.

The plight of refugees is one that both persists to this day and stretches back throughout human history. In 722 BC, the ten tribes of Israel were overwhelmed by the Assyrian army and most of the people were forced out of Israel and resettled far from home (2 Kings 17:24–25). In 605 BC, the same thing happened to the two tribes living in Judah when the Babylonian army conquered Jerusalem and hauled the Jewish leaders to Babylon (2 Chronicles 36:12–20). Then in 139 BC, all of the Jews were expelled from Rome because of their aggressive missionary tactics. In AD 19, Emperor Tiberius once again expelled the Jews in Rome for a similar reason. So it's not surprising that sometime between AD 49 and 51, the Roman Emperor Claudius decreed that all Jews living in Rome had to leave the country. A husband and wife in Rome, whom we'll soon meet in Corinth, were among those being deported. And as we will also soon see, their deportation would be important for the apostle Paul.

Paul was in Athens, waiting for Silas and Timothy to catch up with him (Acts 17:16). Because his preaching in Berea had resulted in so many converts, angry Jews in Thessalonica had come to Berea to make trouble for him. To protect him, the new Berean Christians had hustled Paul off to Athens while Silas and Timothy stayed behind to strengthen the new believers in their understanding of the gospel. So, as we saw in the previous chapter, Paul was alone in Athens. After his fruitful work there, the apostle then made his way—perhaps by sea this time—to Corinth (Acts 18:1). Another new city. Another new set of problems to solve and strategies to implement. One change after another.

Corinth! It's hard to imagine two cities as different from one another as first-century Athens and Corinth. A bit about Corinth's history and geography can help us grasp what made that city so different. Historically, though Corinth had been a Greek city in ancient times, in 146 BC it was defeated in war by the Romans. Later, in 44 BC the city was reestablished as a Roman colony with new settlers (non-Greeks) brought in from other parts of the Empire. In that way, Corinth was reoriented to Roman ideology and organization, and Latin became the official language (though some of the Corinthians continued using Greek). As British New Testament scholar David Horrell tells us, the Corinth Paul visited was a place of "hybrid identities, where Greek culture, language and religion were reshaped in a variety of ways by Roman colonization."[1]

Geographically, Corinth sat on and controlled an isthmus, a narrow land bridge (varying from four to seventeen miles wide) that joined the main part of Greece on the northeast to the Peloponnesus, the large peninsula on the southwest. The Mediterranean Sea around the southern coast of that peninsula was so turbulent that seamen avoided having to sail through it at all costs. So ships that needed to get from the Saronic Gulf on the east to the Ionian Sea on the west (or vice versa) were dragged on log rollers across the land bridge and relaunched on the other side. (Can you see that picture in your imagination?)

Corinth straddled that land bridge with ports on both coasts. This allowed city officials to control taxation on cargo and on the folks whose task it was to pull those boats to either destination port over the logs laid out on the stone-paved roadway. So Corinth was a polyglot with sailors and travelers from every part of the Roman Empire who needed lodging, food, supplies—and prostitutes—while their ships were dragged across the isthmus. In sum, Corinth was a very busy cosmopolitan city controlling all the traffic between the western and eastern ports.

Religiously, virtually every kind of deity had a place of worship there. This included the gods and goddesses from Greece and Rome, the Egyptian deities Isis and Serapis, gods from farther east, as well as local deities and homegrown heroes. In the midst of all that religion, the city was also known for its sexual promiscuity and perversions, problems we see reflected in Paul's letters to the Corinthian Christians. It was into this city dominated, not by philosophers as in Athens, but by international commerce and an even broader range of religious cults, that Paul arrived alone.

COLLEAGUES AND MINISTRY COMPANIONS IN CORINTH

Have you ever wondered how people like Paul supported themselves in all their travels? They had needs for food and lodging and could not assume that people would always take them in. Now for the first time in Acts we learn that the apostle Paul had a trade making leather tents (Acts 18:3). Although Paul had arrived in Corinth alone, he soon found a Christian couple, refugees who had previously been forced from their home in Rome:

Paul left Athens and went to Corinth. There he became acquainted with a Jew named Aquila, born in Pontus, who had recently arrived from Italy with his wife, Priscilla. They had left Italy when Claudius Caesar deported all Jews from Rome. (ACTS 18:1–3)

Aquila was a Jew born in Pontus, a territory on Turkey's Black Sea shore, a long distance from Italy. So how did he come to be deported from Rome? Pontus was originally a Persian province that had been conquered by the Greeks, then later by the Romans. While Rome allowed Pontic kings to rule their territory for many years, in AD 62 Nero forced its king to abdicate his throne. Meanwhile, the Roman soldiers stationed in Pontus were kept busy controlling a sometimes-rebellious populace. The Bible doesn't tell us exactly how Aquila, a Jew from Pontus, ended up in Rome. Scholars suggest that in some of the skirmishes between Roman soldiers and Pontic patriots, he may have been taken prisoner and was later hauled to Rome as a slave. However he got there, students of the Scriptures speculate that he was eventually freed, remained in Rome, worked as a tentmaker, and subsequently married a high-born Gentile woman named Priscilla.[2] What we *do* know from the biblical text is that this couple was among those Jewish refugees who were expelled from Rome by Emperor Claudius. Forced to leave their home, they moved to the closest foreign port, Corinth. To support themselves, they built their tent-making business in Corinth, where the apostle Paul then met and joined them.

Tent-making in the first century was a major industry. Skilled tentmakers would have had steady work supplying the Roman government with leather tents for the myriad military outposts throughout the Empire, as well as selling to civilians and merchants who were on the move. Had Paul been in a trade turning canvas into tents or ship sails, he would have had to carry cumbersome equipment such as a loom. But as a leatherworker, he likely carried only a sharp knife, an awl, and a big curved needle—tools that would fit into a bag the size of a book. His was a good trade for an itinerant missionary.

But Paul's purpose in Corinth was not to earn a living (necessary, but not central). It was to make Jesus Christ known in that pagan corner of the world. As was his habit, Paul spent each Sabbath at the synagogue, "trying to convince the Jews and Greeks alike" (Acts 18:4). However, we also see a shift in Paul's approach: "When [the Jews] opposed him and insulted him, Paul shook the dust from his clothes and said, 'Your blood is upon your own heads—I am innocent. From now on I will go preach to the Gentiles'" (Acts 18:6). Switching the focus of his evangelistic efforts from Jews to Gentiles was a major change in Paul's missionary strategy.[3]

When Paul met Priscilla and Aquila, he learned that they had known and worked with the apostle Peter back in Rome. Early converts to Christ, they were now well experienced in ministry. In leading the refugees Priscilla and Aquila to settle in Corinth, God's Spirit had not only given Paul colleagues who shared his trade and so provided a means of self-support, but had also given him coworkers in the gospel who would stand side-by-side with him in ministry. They were God's gift to this tireless but sometimes tired apostle.

PRISCILLA AND AQUILA, PAUL'S "COWORKERS" IN MINISTRY

In the book of Acts and in Paul's letters, we meet this tent-making couple, Priscilla and Aquila, in three different cities. As already noted, they connected with Paul first in *Corinth* and worked with him there in both ministry and tent-making for around eighteen months (AD 50–52).

Paul then took Priscilla and Aquila with him when he headed across the Aegean Sea to *Ephesus* in southwestern Turkey. Because Paul had made a vow that required a trip to Jerusalem, he left the couple in Ephesus to establish their work. It was during Paul's absence that they encountered Apollos, an eloquent Jewish speaker, knowledgeable in the Old Testament Scriptures. This dynamic preacher in the Ephesian synagogue "knew only about John's baptism" (Acts 18:25). When they learned that about him, Priscilla and Aquila took him aside and taught him more fully about Jesus as the way of God.

When his vow was completed, Paul returned to Ephesus, settling in with Priscilla and Aquila for a difficult but fruitful three-year ministry effort in that city. During those years, he wrote his first letter to the Corinthians, noting, "The churches here in the province of Asia [Turkey] send greetings in the Lord, as do Aquila and Priscilla and all the others who gather in their home for church meetings" (1 Corinthians 16:19).

Finally, at the end of Paul's letter to the Romans, we discover that Priscilla and Aquila were now back in *Rome*. Obviously, the ban on Jews in Rome had been lifted and the couple had returned home. But true to form, they kept busy starting new churches. Paul greeted them there with these words:

> Give my greetings to Priscilla and Aquila, my co-workers in the ministry of Christ Jesus. In fact, they once risked their lives for me. I am thankful to them, and so are all the Gentile churches. Also give my greetings to the church that meets in their home. (Romans 16:3–5)

Note what Paul said about them in that greeting. First, he counted them as his coworkers in ministry. Second, they had at some point risked their own lives for Paul (probably in Ephesus). Third, a new church was now meeting in their home. Few people had worked with Paul more than they had: for eighteen months in Corinth, and then for three years in Ephesus. He had good reason to call them his coworkers.

But what precisely did it mean to be a coworker with the apostle Paul? Was a coworker a subordinate, the equivalent of an assistant running errands and fetching coffee for the apostle? Or was a coworker something more, perhaps even next in line to the apostle as a kind of vice-president apostle? Or was that person actually an equal, working side-by-side with the apostle, doing virtually the same tasks? In both tent-making and in evangelism, in both Corinth and in Ephesus, Aquila and Priscilla were in every sense of the word Paul's coworkers. They worked side-by-side with the apostle, doing whatever he was doing.

The Greek word translated "coworker" is *sunergon*. It is a word Paul uses to describe eleven different people:

- Philemon (Philemon 1:1)
- Timothy (1 Thessalonians 3:2)

- Aristarchus, Mark, and Justus (Colossians 4:10–11)
- Titus (2 Corinthians 8:23)
- Urbanus (Romans 16:9)
- Euodia and Syntyche (Philippians 4:2–3)
- Priscilla and Aquila (Romans 16:3–5)

Note that three of the eleven are women: Euodia, Syntyche, and Priscilla. Paul makes no distinction between them and their male counterparts—all are described as his coworkers.

Of the six times that Priscilla and Aquila are mentioned in the New Testament, four times Priscilla's name came first. We could write that off as random or perhaps simply as a courtesy to her as a woman. But New Testament scholars tell us that in first-century writings, the ordering of names was never random, and the first-named person was usually the one recognized as having more prominence in ministry.[4]

THIS TEAM WAS NOT STOPPED BY STRESSFUL EVENTS

As we follow Priscilla and Aquila from Rome to Corinth, from Corinth to Ephesus, and then from Ephesus back to Rome, we're struck with the major adaptations this couple had to make with each move. We seldom think of them as refugees in Corinth, but that was their status. From the citadel of Roman culture, they landed in Corinth, a polyglot commercial town populated by freed slaves from every corner of the Empire.

What had they left behind as they went into involuntary exile? We know from Roman archeological finds that Priscilla was high-born, with a house on the property of her relative Pudens (2 Timothy 4:21), a Roman senator and a man of great wealth. Even though Aquila is thought by scholars to have probably been a freed slave from Pontus, that in no way proves that he was Priscilla's inferior. First-century slaves were often very well educated and respected for professional-level skills. Frequently, they functioned in important government positions or as sought-after scholars. If we think even for a minute about the downward dislocation of this couple as they were evicted from Rome, we begin to grasp the enormity of their losses. Yet, nothing in the biblical text leads us to think that they sat around commiserating with one another about those losses. Instead, we find them setting up housekeeping in Corinth in a dwelling large enough to accommodate the apostle Paul as a resident. In time, that house also served as the center for the newly forming church.

Nor do we catch them grumbling when, at the end of their eighteen-month stint planting churches in Corinth, the apostle Paul took them with him to Ephesus to start the same process again. This meant new adjustments in a town very different from Corinth. Just as Paul had not quibbled with the Holy Spirit about leaving Turkey and beginning new ministries in Greece, Priscilla and Aquila appear to have taken each move in stride, seeing the leading of God's Spirit in each. They had not asked for exile from Rome, but once in Corinth, they could set up shop making leather tents in association with Paul, and they could reach out to people unlike themselves with the truth of God's love and salvation. From a lavish home on Rome's famous Aventine to whatever rented housing could be found in either Corinth or Ephesus, Priscilla and Aquila took what was available, thanked God, and made the best of each new situation.

When the apostle Paul landed in Corinth, he needed a means of earning an income to support his work, and he also needed the support of seasoned Christian workers. God supplied that need in a way that had greatly inconvenienced Priscilla and Aquila—expulsion from Rome by the Emperor. Perhaps because the large city of Corinth was just across the Adriatic Sea from Italy and would provide a place to set up their tent-making business, they chose to move there. But can we discern the hand of God in their decision? I think so.

God's Spirit Can Use Stressful Events to Guide Us

Understandably, we are most comfortable in familiar surroundings. We don't like the inconvenience of being uprooted. That "uprooting" might be any number of things—a ruptured friendship, the loss of employment, an unwanted move to a distant place, a sudden illness, or the death of someone we love. And on and on. The list is long of ways in which stress can move into our lives and send us reeling. How do we deal with our "refugee" status in any of those forms? Can we see ways in which God can work through those experiences when they threaten to knock us down? Can we visualize any benefit accruing from stressful events that hit us?

As noted previously in chapter 5, the apostle Paul reminded the Roman Christians that "God causes everything to work together for the good of those who love God and are called according to his purpose for them" (Romans 8:28). Priscilla and Aquila knew that and it kept them upright and moving forward when hit by all the unwanted problems of exile. Just as he did for them, God's Spirit can be trusted to work through our stressful experiences for our good. It is often in such times that God opens doors for us that we might not otherwise have considered.

So what attitude do we bring to those stressful events that come our way in life? I live in New England, not far from wonderful beaches curbing the Atlantic Ocean. If I go to the beach, I have three options. I can stay on shore, enjoying the warm sand and avoiding the water entirely. Or I can ease into the shallow water, no more than waist-deep. As ocean waves roll toward me, I can face those waves, running into them with delight. Or I can turn my back to them, hurrying to the shore to avoid them.

Life doesn't always allow us to sit on the beach and admire the sea from a safe distance. At times, we find ourselves waist-deep in situations that feel dangerous. Can we face them with confidence that God's Spirit will hold us and lead us and stay with us through those tough times? That's when God's Spirit whispers, *Yes, you can trust me. I'm there to support you in every trial.* You can rest in that reality because God is really there for you.

• • •

QUESTIONS FOR PERSONAL REFLECTION OR GROUP DISCUSSION

1. To be a refugee is to be forced from one's home and to suffer the stresses of loss, relocation, and starting over. It's a dynamic that we can also experience to a lesser degree whenever we are uprooted by stressful experiences. In what ways, if any, would you say you have "refugee" status in this season of your life? What loss, dislocation, or new reality are you facing?

2. One of the gifts God gave to Paul as well as Priscilla and Aquila was the gift of each other. They shared a home, tent-making work, and a ministry that made them coworkers. It was an intimate and shared life in every way. What appeals to you about this kind of shared home, work, and ministry life? Have you ever experienced anything like it, or would you want to? Share the reasons for your response.

3. Based on what you learned about Paul, Priscilla, and Aquila, how would you describe what it might mean to be a "coworker" in ministry today? (Note that ministry includes any and all the ways you routinely and intentionally love and serve others in Jesus's name.)

4. If you could have a true coworker relationship in ministry, in what ways do you imagine it would it be similar to or different from experiences you've had or are currently having in ministry?

7

Phoebe
God's Spirit Guides Us
as Servant Leaders

In the 1970s our family lived in Europe, but three of our four children were in college in the States. At that time, the per-minute costs for international telephone calls were prohibitively high, which meant they were out of the question except for emergencies. Instead, we communicated by letter, now known as snail-mail. We bought tissue-thin "airforms" from the post office. These allowed us to type our letters from edge to edge, filling the short one-page airforms as full as possible. (Yes, we also used an old-fashioned typewriter.) When the airform was sent off, it usually took ten days for our family in the USA to receive it. Then, if our son or our daughters wrote back at once, it would be another ten days before we received their reply. We usually figured on a minimum of three weeks to complete any two-way communication.

Now technology has brought us instant communication. With just a few clicks, we can reach someone almost anywhere in the world with a text or an email. We can connect face-to-face in real time with apps like Skype, choose among multiple options for posting our pictures and personal news on Facebook, or instantly air our choice opinions on Twitter. The ease of instant communication today makes it hard for many folks to imagine what it was like forty or fifty years ago when we didn't even have mobile phones, much less smartphones.

Now consider the apostle Paul's dilemma when he finished composing his important letter to the Christians in Rome. He was more than 700 miles away in Corinth and a lot of seawater separated him from Italy and the letter's recipients. Ships were designed to transport merchandise rather than passengers, seas were turbulent, and shipping often stopped altogether during the winter. So how was he to get his letter to the Christians in Rome?

This document was particularly precious because it was the only copy. Paul had no photocopier, no external hard drive, and no Cloud from which to retrieve a new copy. At sixteen chapters, it was one of Paul's longest, most detailed letters and had no doubt required many sheets of parchment or papyrus. Parchment (thin sheets of goatskin or sheepskin) lasted longer, but much of the time only papyrus sheets were available. They were made from the pithy stalks of the papyrus plant and were much more fragile. Writing on either was time-consuming, and a letter lost would be impossible to re-create. Needless to say, the stakes were high. Paul needed someone he could trust to hand-deliver his letter.

SPECIAL DELIVERY FROM CORINTH

Fortunately, this wasn't Paul's first stint in Corinth. On his previous missionary journey, he had spent eighteen months in Corinth preaching to men and women about Jesus Christ. During those months of preaching and teaching, house churches were formed in different parts of sprawling Corinth and its suburbs, which meant Paul likely had many contacts throughout the region. Now Paul was back in Corinth for a third time, checking on the spiritual health of the churches in that city, including a church in the eastern suburb of Cenchrea. It was here that he drafted his long letter to the Christians in Rome.

Talking one day with Phoebe, one of the leaders in the Cenchrean church, he learned that she planned to make a trip to Rome. I imagine their conversation went something like this:

Paul:　Phoebe, did you just say that you're going to Rome?

Phoebe: Yes, it's necessary for my business. But it's hard to find a merchant vessel captain willing to let me purchase passage.

Paul:　If only ships had more room for passengers. Most of the time, especially on my trips from Ephesus to Caesarea, I've had to camp out on the deck, and sometimes the ship's captain isn't even willing to allow that.

Phoebe (laughing): That's true. And the captains that do allow it can charge an astronomical price for a ticket. Plus, there are the other costs—buying food, bedding, even a small tent if I want any privacy onboard. But you know all of this already. Why are you asking me about my trip? Are you thinking about going back to Rome as well?

Paul: No, but I'm about to complete a long letter to the Christians in Rome, and I don't yet have a way to get it to them.

Phoebe: Oh, in that case, I could carry it to Rome for you—if you would trust me with it.

Paul: Of course I would trust you with it. But we both know the dangers of sailing in these seas.

Phoebe: Dangers, yes. Hardly a week passes that I don't hear of some ship capsizing in a storm with all of the cargo and crew lost. But it's not just the dangers that we have to think about. It's also the *time* it takes for any kind of crossing. I need a ship to take me from Corinth to Italy's port at Ostia. Military ships have oarsmen to row the ship forward, but we're completely dependent on the wind to fill our sails. The prevailing winds are rarely in our favor when traveling west. I face a long sea voyage, not just in distance but also in hours spent when the wind is against us.

Paul: So what are your plans, Phoebe?

Phoebe: I've been in touch with several captains whose ships are in port. One captain plans to sail in ten days. If there's still room on his ship after all the Rome-bound merchandise has been loaded, I may be able to purchase a ticket. It's not certain that I'll get passage on that ship, but it's looking hopeful. So give me your letter to the Roman Christians, but be sure to wrap it well so I can keep it dry during the voyage. Between storms and waves that may wash over the deck, it needs to be protected if you want it to arrive intact.

Paul: Thank you, Phoebe. My prayers will be with you as you travel. You're in God's hands.

Phoebe: Good hands, to be sure.

Phoebe did indeed make the long, slow journey from Corinth to Rome, where she delivered Paul's letter safely to the Christians there. Now imagine her sitting with the others as the letter was read aloud to the congregation meeting in the home of Priscilla and Aquila. As the reader neared the end of the letter, he came to these words:

I commend to you our sister Phoebe, who is a deacon in the church in Cenchrea. Welcome her in the Lord as one who is worthy of honor among God's people. Help her in whatever she needs, for she has been helpful to many, and especially to me. (ROMANS 16:1–2)

"Welcome her in the Lord as one who is worthy of honor among God's people." Paul introduced his friend to the Roman Christians "as one who is worthy of honor." With that brief phrase, Paul established Phoebe's ministry credentials.

UNDERSTANDING THE ROLE OF DEACON

The first thing we know about Phoebe is that she was a deacon in the church in Cenchrea, a suburb of Corinth.

Some Bible translations call her a "servant," but the Greek word is *diakonos* from which our word "deacon" comes. At the same time, the notion of the role of deacon was also one of service. Recall that early in the book of Acts, rumblings of discontent had erupted among the Christians in Jerusalem: the Greek-speaking believers complained that the Hebrew-speaking believers were discriminating against the Greek widows "in the daily distribution of food" (Acts 6:1). The Greek word there translated "distribution" is *diakonia*. Distributing food to the needy was one aspect of "deaconing." To solve the problem, the disciples appointed seven men (most of whom were Greek) to make sure the Greek widows were fed every day.

But the duties and responsibilities of a deacon most likely included more than such acts of service. Recall that Stephen and Philip were two of the seven appointed to make sure the Greek widows had food. In the verses immediately following their appointment to this act of service, Stephen is described as "a man full of God's grace and power, [who] performed amazing miracles and signs among the people" (Acts 6:8). Stephen was out on the streets or in the marketplace preaching and healing with power from God. In the midst of exciting ministry, Stephen was brought before the Jewish High Council. There, he preached a sermon that led directly to his martyrdom by stoning (Acts 7:59–60). Deacon Stephen was active in many forms of ministry.

Deacon Philip, too, was active as an evangelist. Persecution in Jerusalem had driven many Christians out of the city, and Philip landed in Samaria where, "Crowds listened intently to Philip because they were eager to hear his message and see the miraculous signs he did. Many evil spirits were cast out, screaming as they left their victims. And many who had been paralyzed or lame were healed" (Acts 8:6–7). Obviously, the ministry work connected to the position of deacon included much more than feeding widows.

When we turn to Paul's letters, we learn that the apostle used the word *diakonos* to describe five people. First, he used it to describe his own ministry (Ephesians 3:7; Colossians 1:23). He also used it to describe the ministry of four other people:

- Timothy (1 Thessalonians 3:2; 1 Timothy 4:6)
- Tychicus (Ephesians 6:21; Colossians 4:7)
- Ephaphras (Colossians 1:7)
- Phoebe (Romans 16:1–2)

Whatever the apostle Paul and the other three men were doing in ministry, Phoebe is likely to have been doing in the Cenchrean church. Note that Paul didn't call Phoebe a *diakonesse*, meaning a female deacon. He used *diakonos,* the same title for her that he used for himself and for his three other male coworkers.

If Paul makes no distinction between the ministries of male and female deacons, why have so many others throughout church history consistently done so? Perhaps the most significant factor in the last four hundred years can be traced back to a source that might surprise you: Bible translators.

Sometimes Bible translators allow their own biases to influence their word choice. For example, back in 1608 when King James of England authorized a new translation of the Bible (which we know today as the King James Version), translators consistently rendered *diakonos* as "minister" for the four men, but as "servant" for Phoebe. Whatever else we know about Phoebe, Paul, Timothy, Tychicus, and Ephaphras, if deacon Phoebe was a servant, then deacon Paul and deacon Timothy and deacon Tychicus and deacon Ephaphras were also servants. While we don't know the full range of tasks first-century deacons carried out, we can say it was a role that described at least a part of Phoebe's ministry in the same terms used to describe a part of Paul's work.

The issue of deacons came up in Paul's first letter to Timothy. Here is how he discussed some of the requirements for deacons:

> In the same way, deacons must be well respected and have integrity. They must not be heavy drinkers or dishonest with money. They must be committed to the mystery of the faith now revealed and must live with a clear conscience. Before they are appointed deacons, let them be closely examined. If they pass the test, let them serve as deacons. (1 TIMOTHY 3:8–10)

At this point, depending on which translation you might be reading, you may conclude when you get to verse 11, that Paul is writing only about male deacons because this verse describes the requirements for "their wives."

> In the same way, their wives must be respected and must not slander others. They must exercise self-control and be faithful in everything they do. (1 TIMOTHY 3:11)

It's important to note that the Greek word translated here as "wives" is the same word used for "women." Therefore, many biblical scholars[1] regard verse 11 as referring not to deacons' wives, but to women in church office, in which case, the verse would read, "In the same way, women

[deacons] must be respected and must not slander others."
The Greek text in verse 11 exactly parallels Paul's phrasing
and observations in verse 8:

> "In the same way, [male] deacons [*diakonous hosautos*]
> must be well respected . . ." (verse 8).
> "In the same way, [women] [*gynaikas hosautos*] must be
> respected . . ." (verse 11).

Other scholars also point out that if the word "women"
in verse 11 refers to "wives," it's hard to explain why
there are no similar qualifications given for the wives of
church leaders in 1 Timothy 3:1–7. Furthermore, it would
be strange for anyone (man or woman) who was not an
officeholder to be required to meet practically the identical
qualifications, listed in the same order, as the qualifications
for deacons listed in 1 Timothy 3:8.[2] We also must ask, if
Paul didn't condone women deacons, why did he introduce
Phoebe to the Roman Christians as "deacon of the church
in Cenchrea" (Romans 16:1)?

Apparently, the first-generation churches made no distinction between the roles and responsibilities of male and
female deacons. But later theologians and church leaders,
who were influenced by the culture around them, did—
sometimes in what might seem like surprising ways. Ancient
pagan cultures had always been spooked about menstruation: how was it that a woman could bleed every month and
not die? It was a notion that also gripped some churchmen.
The conclusion was that women must have a power that is
evil and destructive. Though pagan in origin, such cultural
attitudes could well have passed into Judaism and then into
Christianity.

A bishop of Alexandria, Dionysius the Great (birth year unknown, died AD 264), was the first Christian leader to urge that women not be allowed to approach the altar (or even to enter the church) while menstruating. By AD 300, only virgins or widows over sixty could serve as deacons, and their tasks were then limited to keeping the church from scandal in a hostile culture, visiting sick women in their homes, and finding seats for women in church.

The Church Father Tertullian (circa AD 155–240) introduced two changes in the third century that are with us still. While Paul referred to the early Christian churches as "the family of faith" (Galatians 6:10) or "the household of God" (Ephesians 2:19 ESV), Tertullian shifted to a governmental model, much like the Roman Empire. Paul envisioned ministry in the Body of Christ as everyone bringing his or her gift in service to the church, but Tertullian saw ministry roles as positions of power with corresponding legal rights. In short, he created a pecking order within ministry that ultimately separated clergy from laity.

Tertullian's other significant action came out of his belief that "it is not permitted to a woman to speak in church, but neither is it permitted her to teach, nor to baptize, nor to offer, nor to claim for herself a lot in any manly function not to say [in any] sacerdotal office."[3] In short, he declared that women could not hold any kind of office in the church.

But he didn't stop there: sexuality had become a huge issue for him and other churchmen. In the end, they determined that Christian women were responsible not only for their own chastity, but also for that of men. If a woman in any way excited a man's imagination sexually, the woman, not the man, was considered the sinful party. From there, a negative theology of female personhood evolved, based on the notion that from Eve onward, women were responsible for sin in the world. As a consequence, they must be kept out of sight where they couldn't tempt men. The idea was that the spiritual well-being of a man could be compromised by a woman.

These beliefs dominated ideas about women throughout the Middle Ages, and while the Reformation and more recent movements have mitigated such beliefs, the belief in the basic inferiority of women has survived into our own day. Of course, not all Christians accept that as true, but its presence in some quarters may explain why some translators tread lightly when dealing with this text.

Does any of this historical background help us understand why translators even today might shy away from implying that a woman could be a deacon?

It's time to return to Phoebe, identified by Paul as both a deacon (*diakonos*) and as "*prostatis*." Our translation has called her a "benefactor." We've already met benefactors in earlier chapters, so we know something about them. Is this an accurate description of Phoebe, or does *prostatis* carry different freight?

PHOEBE AS *PROSTATIS*

In introducing Phoebe to the Roman Christians, Paul first names her a deacon (*diakonos*) and then says of her, "she has been *helpful* to many, and especially to me" (Romans 16:2, emphasis added). In the Greek, the word "helpful" is actually a noun, *prostatis*. This is why some translators refer to Phoebe as a "helper," a "patron," a "benefactor," or a "succourer."

But what precisely is a *prostatis*? The biblical scholar and lexicographer Joseph Thayer defines the first meaning of this Greek word as "a woman set over others."[4] It is the feminine form of a noun describing a leader. In the early second century, Christian apologist Justin Martyr used the masculine form, *prostates*, to describe the president or presiding officer of a local church, a person who preaches, teaches, or presides at the Lord's table.[5]

When Paul refers to Phoebe as *prostatis* in Romans 16:2, it could be that he is essentially encouraging those in Rome to welcome her because, "she has been a helpful leader of many, and especially me." Even the conservative Bible scholar Charles Ryrie, who taught that the role of women in church is "not a leading one," acknowledged that *prostatis* "includes some kind of leadership."[6]

While the singular feminine noun *prostatis* occurs only here in the New Testament, it comes from the verb *proistemi,* a common word in Paul's letters. So let's consider a few examples of how Paul uses other forms of the word elsewhere.

- When speaking about the various gifts God gives, Paul writes, "If God has given you leadership [*proistemenos*] ability, take the responsibility seriously" (Romans 12:8).

- In the closing remarks of his first letter to the church at Thessalonica, Paul writes, "honor those who are your leaders [*proistemenous*] in the Lord's work" (1 Thessalonians 5:12).

- When providing advice to his protégé Timothy, Paul writes, "Elders [*proestotes*] who do their work well should be respected and paid well, especially those who work hard at both preaching and teaching" (1 Timothy 5:17).

In sum, it seems clear that as Paul presents her, Phoebe was both a deacon and a leader in the church in Cenchrea. Paul knew her well and trusted her with his precious letter to the Christians in Rome. God's Spirit had led the apostle to write his important letter to the Romans and God's Spirit had led in Phoebe's travel plans so that she could carry the letter safely to its destination.

LEADERSHIP IN GOD'S UPSIDE-DOWN KINGDOM

Does God's Spirit call women into leadership positions in the church today? Before answering that question, consider that Jesus had some surprisingly upside-down notions about leadership. When the mother of James and John asked Jesus to give her two sons privileged places in his Kingdom, his response to all of the disciples was to stress the connection between leadership and service:

> "You know that the rulers in this world lord it over their people, and officials flaunt their authority over those under them. But among you it will be different. Whoever wants to be a leader among you must be your servant, and who-ever wants to be first among you must become your slave. For even the Son of Man came not to be served but to serve others and to give his life as a ransom for many." (MATTHEW 20:25–28)

Do you recall the event recorded by the apostle John during the last meal Jesus and his followers shared before his arrest?

[Jesus] got up from the table, took off his robe, wrapped a towel around his waist, and poured water into a basin. Then he began to wash the disciples' feet, drying them with the towel he had around him. . . . After washing their feet, he put on his robe again and sat down and asked, "Do you understand what I was doing? You call me 'Teacher' and 'Lord,' and you are right, because that's what I am. And since I, your Lord and Teacher, have washed your feet, you ought to wash each other's feet. I have given you an example to follow. Do as I have done to you. . . . Now that you know these things, God will bless you for doing them." (John 13:4–5, 12–15, 17)

Do you remember Jesus's response when Pilate asked him about his kingship?

Jesus answered, "My Kingdom is not an earthly kingdom. If it were, my followers would fight to keep me from being handed over to the Jewish leaders. But my Kingdom is not of this world." (John 18:36)

Throughout his actions and his teachings recorded in the four gospels, Jesus lands counterpunch after counterpunch on the world's ideas about power and authority. God's Kingdom is upside-down to all the prevailing ideas about leadership. It turns out that the old idea from church history that the deaconate was preparation for church leadership is on track, but misunderstood. A deacon is called to be a servant, and servanthood is the best preparation for leadership.

Do you see how Jesus turns our notions about leadership upside-down? His consistent message was that the way most people think about power and dominance is not God's way of thinking. Paul understood that, which is why he could write:

> God chose things the world considers foolish in order to shame those who think they are wise. And he chose things that are powerless to shame those who are powerful. God chose things despised by the world, things counted as nothing at all, and used them to bring to nothing what the world considers important. As a result, no one can ever boast in the presence of God. (1 CORINTHIANS 1:27–29)

Does it make sense to you that God chooses "the things that are powerless" to shame those with power? Or that God obliterates—totally annihilates—"what the world considers important"? Paul then nails the reason for the "upside-down-ness" of God's Kingdom: it's so that we can't brag about what we've accomplished. Whatever gifts Phoebe brought to the church in Cenchrea, she was there as God's servant. No room for boasting. It is in serving that we lead. Leadership is from the bottom, not from the top.

So back to our question: Does God's Spirit call women into leadership positions in the church today? It depends on both the woman and the ministry situation. Concerning the woman, does she have the necessary gifts for ministry? Does she have the passion, the vision, the temperament, and the drive for it? Concerning the ministry situation, is it one in which she may use her gifts and passion in Christ's service? Is the ministry situation the right place for the gifts God has given her? Above all, does she have the humility to know that whatever God accomplishes through her service, it is ultimately *God* at work?

Behind those questions lurks yet another: Does she see

ministry as a place to serve or as a position of power? In God's upside-down Kingdom, only those with servant hearts are fit for leadership. And this applies to men in leadership as well as to women.

Think about Phoebe: she was *diakonos*, a minister with a servant heart; she was also *prostatis*, someone God had gifted to stand before others as their leader. It takes both qualities together for ministry: only one with a servant heart can stand before others as their leader.

Phoebe successfully carried out her mission for Paul. Once again, imagine her sitting with the Christians in Rome in the home of Priscilla and Aquila. After a long and difficult journey, she has completed her task. Can you see her smile as the letter is read and Paul names different men and women in the room with whom he had worked somewhere in the Roman Empire?

Can you imagine yourself sitting there, listening to Paul's letter being read to first-century Christians? You might glance around the room, taking in Priscilla and Aquila, remembering all they endured as exiles, yet planting churches in Corinth and Ephesus. Here, they mix in with Christian slaves and highbrow Romans, serving the body of Christ out of love for each one in that room. There's the apostle Peter in the corner, listening appreciatively to the godly wisdom Paul had written to his people in Rome. No self-importance there! Just one more follower of Jesus leading by serving. This is the family of faith. This is the household of God. Together, these men and women are part of an upside-down Kingdom that is not of this world.

Our imagination may take us back to first-century Rome momentarily, but the rest of the time we live in the twenty-first century. So how do I think of leadership? How do you think of leadership? Is it not leadership unless it has all the trappings of power around it? Or does it make sense that true leadership is grounded in our service?

God's Spirit puts a completely different spin on what leadership is about. Whether our service is to fill the communion cups or to stand in front of the congregation and serve it, we lead. Whether we teach the Scriptures each Sunday or listen to a senior citizen repeat the same tale for the umpteenth time, we lead. In God's upside-down Kingdom, we lead as we serve. Our service speaks volumes to those around us. It may even be what God's Spirit will use to change their lives. Ultimately, that is true leadership.

• • •

QUESTIONS FOR PERSONAL REFLECTION OR GROUP DISCUSSION

1. If you could have a conversation with Phoebe, what kinds of things would you ask her? What would you most like to know about her life, her relationship with Paul, her journey to Rome, or her ministry as a deacon? Why?

2. Overall, would you say this chapter challenged your views or supported your views on what the Bible teaches about women as deacons? Share the reasons for your response.

3. If it's true that first-generation churches made no distinction between the roles and responsibilities of male and female deacons, what implications might that have for both men and women in the church today? What implications might it have for you—for your understanding of the role of deacon, or for the ministry God has called you to in this season of life?

4. How would you describe the prevailing views about leadership within your own Christian community? In what ways do these views reflect or fail to reflect Jesus's teaching about the upside-down nature of leadership in the Kingdom?

8

Junia[s] and Andronicus
God's Spirit Guides Us through Early Experiences We Did Not Value

Perhaps you're familiar with the popular murder-mystery board game *Clue*. It's 1926, and six people have gathered for a weekend in an English country house when a murder takes place. Which of the guests did it? Where did it happen? And what was the weapon used? Solving the crime requires sorting through six potential murderers, six possible weapons, and nine rooms in which the murder could have taken place. Was it Professor Plum using the candlestick in the dining room? Or could it have been Mrs. Peacock using the wrench in the conservatory? What about Colonel Mustard using the rope in the study?

Whether we're playing *Clue* or reading a good mystery novel, we know that in solving the crime, everything depends on the hints or clues planted here and there. We're drawn in, scratching our heads about clues that seem to contradict one another, wondering how we'll ever find the solution that puts all the pieces of the puzzle together in the right way.

Although he wasn't writing a murder-mystery, the apostle Paul created a puzzle that has baffled many Bible scholars over the years. The puzzle concerns his mention of a mystery couple in his letter to the church at Rome. He wrote just two lines:

> Greet Andronicus and Junia[s], my fellow Jews, who were in prison with me. They are highly respected among the apostles and became followers of Christ before I did. (ROMANS 16:7)

It's not a lot to go on, but it does provide some clues. Here is a list of the clues we have about this couple:

1. We know their names: Andronicus and Junia[s].

2. We know they were Jews.

3. We know they were in prison with the apostle Paul.

4. We know they were highly respected among the apostles.

5. And we know they became followers of Christ before Paul was converted.

But this is the first and only time in the Bible that we meet them, and so we have no way to fit them into what we think we know about the apostles.

Based on Paul's statement, that might look like the complete list of available clues, but wait—there is actually a sixth clue, one we can derive from other available information:

6. If they were apostles, we know that one criterion for apostleship was that the person had "seen Jesus" during Jesus's earthly ministry (1 Corinthians 9:1; 15:6–9).

Were Andronicus and Junia[s] among the five hundred (1 Corinthians 15:6) who had seen Jesus at one time after his resurrection, but before his ascension? In his first letter to the Corinthian Christians, Paul had said that most of those who were in that group of five hundred were still alive, though some had died. If they weren't part of that crowd, then where might they have "seen Jesus"? And if they had seen Jesus, how did they fit into his earthly life and ministry?

And then there are those names: Andronicus and Junia[s]. These are such Roman names, not Jewish at all. But Paul calls them "his fellow Jews." However, just as he had two names—the Roman name Paul as well as his Jewish name Saul—these folks may well have previously been known by Jewish names while still back in Palestine. But what were those names? Searching our memory of the four Gospel accounts of Jesus's earthly ministry, we are hard-pressed to come up with any that might fit that category.

We thought we knew a lot about Paul's three missionary journeys, but obviously a lot happened that Luke did not record. Somewhere along the line, this mystery couple shared jail-time with Paul. Where? When? Why?

Then again, there's the "apostle" bit. According to my *Oxford American Dictionary*, one definition of an apostle is "the first successful Christian missionary in a country or to a people." Would that fit this mystery couple? Perhaps yes, perhaps no.

From their names, it's clear they weren't among the twelve disciples chosen by Jesus at the outset of his ministry. But Jesus had other apostles. We know that Paul was an apostle (1 Corinthians 9:1), and others also had that title, such as Barnabas, Silas, and Timothy (Acts 14:4; 1 Thessalonians 1:1). We've already touched on one criterion for apostleship: that person must have personally seen Jesus Christ at some point. But the word *apostle* itself simply means "a sent one." This raises even more questions. Who sent this mystery pair? When? And where were they sent? We meet them now in Rome, but how did they get there, and why were they there?

If this mystery couple had become followers of Jesus before the apostle Paul did, were they members of the Jerusalem church (as described in the early chapters of the book of Acts)? If not, were they perhaps Jews from Rome or elsewhere who met Jesus one year when they came to Jerusalem for one of the great Jewish feasts?

So many questions. So few clues.

JUNIA OR JUNIAS?

I have at least eleven different translations of the New Testament on my shelf. None of the translations differ about Andronicus, but they diverge about the second person in that pair. Of the eleven, three designate this second person as "Junias," but eight designate this person as "Junia."[1] So what? What's the big deal about a little "s"? Couldn't it just be a typo? What, if anything, is at stake?

The potential big deal is that the presence or absence of the "s" is the difference between the masculine and feminine versions of the name. Junias is regarded as a masculine Roman name, while Junia was a common Roman woman's name. Scholars tell us that the name Junia occurs more than 250 times in inscriptions in Rome alone, whereas the name

Junias has not been found anywhere. So was Andronicus's companion apostle a man or a woman?

Early church fathers had no problem with that question. Origen (AD 185–253) referred to Junia as a woman, and later Jerome (circa AD 340–420) and others agreed. Archbishop John Chrysostom (circa AD 349–407) wrote, "To be an apostle is something great. But to be outstanding among the apostles, just think what a wonderful song of praise that is! . . . How great the wisdom of this woman must have been that she was even deemed worthy of the title of apostle."[2]

So if the Church Fathers were clear that Junia was a woman, where did the notion of Junias come from? Aegidius of Rome (1245–1316) was the first to refer to Andronicus and Junias as "honorable men." Why would he have done that? From the late Patristic period of church history throughout the Middle Ages, the notion that a woman could be an apostle became increasingly unthinkable. Because it was unthinkable, it was reasoned that Junia must be a man. From the thirteenth century onward, her name was changed to Junias, and she was thereafter referred to as a man. More recently, however, a majority of Bible translators have restored the name to Junia, a woman who was numbered among the apostles. But translation questions still arise. Some argue that, while Junia is definitely a woman, she was merely well known to the apostles. But other biblical scholars are quick to point out that this is not what the grammatical structure of this verse in Greek indicates. The Greek makes it clear that Andronicus and Junia were not merely *known* to the apostles, but were, in fact, *well-known* apostles in their own right.[3]

JUNIA *AND* JOANNA?

We know that Junia was the Roman name of a Jewish apostle. We also know that person must have been one of Jesus's followers, probably named in the Gospels, and must have been present when he sent his followers out into the world as his ambassadors. Who could fit that bill? We get our first clue from the fact that "Junia" is the Roman or Latin equivalent of the Hebrew name "Joanna." Do you remember her?

We first met Joanna in chapter 1. She was part of that group of intrepid women who supported Jesus and his band financially, who were last at the cross and at his burial in the tomb, and then first at the tomb on Easter morning. Joanna (along with Mary of Magdala and Susanna) was one of the women named in Luke 8:1–3 who had received healing from Jesus, and who then became part of his band of disciples traveling around the Galilee and back and forth to Jerusalem in the south for the great Jewish feasts.

As you'll recall, Joanna was the wife of Chuza, King Herod Antipas's finance minister for the realm. We know that Chuza's ethnicity was most likely Nabatean, which could have connected him to Antipas's royal family. Antipas's grandmother was Nabatean, and the king had married a Nabatean princess. Chuza's role was as *epitropos*, as manager of the king's estate. This made him, in effect, the finance minister of Galilee, administering all revenues as well as the royal domains. Chuza was a very high ranking official in the king's court. Because he would need to have gained experience and expertise for that office, he was most likely an older man. As we shall soon see, all of these details provide potentially important clues to help us solve the mystery of Junia's identity.

The royal court was in the new Roman city of Tiberias, which is where scholars believe Joanna's family may have settled. New Testament scholar Richard Bauckham tells us that Joanna herself (certainly Jewish from her name) was most likely a member of one of the leading families of Tiberias or of another powerful Galilean family. So Chuza's marriage to Joanna was probably an alliance between an elite Jewish family and the Roman Herodian court. While some of this is scholarly conjecture, whatever Joanna's family of origin, her marriage to Chuza made her part of the Herodian upper class of Tiberias. Again, all of these are important clues.

Think about her life at court in the light of what Joanna eventually did (according Luke 8:1–3). As noted in chapter 1, when she became a follower of Jesus, she had to cross a huge social gulf. But she willingly set aside her palace life and all its amenities to follow Christ.

For two years, Joanna was in the constant company of Jesus and his followers. Imagine what a learning experience that was—listening to Jesus teach here, there, and everywhere; watching him embrace and lift up the underdogs; seeing the power of God unleashed time and again when people needed food or healing. When Jesus had sent out the Twelve to preach and to heal, these men represented the twelve tribes of Israel (Luke 9:1–6). But when he later sent out seventy-two to preach and to heal, nothing in the text restricts this to men (Luke 10:1–17). Many scholars believe that women were part of that preaching/healing band, and Joanna may have been among them. Imagine her in village marketplaces talking to women as they sold their wares, or watch her touching those in need of healing or encouragement. Was this the same aristocratic lady attached to the royal court in Tiberias?

At this point, you may be wondering how Joanna managed this new lifestyle with her ragtag bunch of friends in light of her marriage to the king's finance minister, Chuza. Recall that marriages for women were arranged when they were still very young, and usually by age fourteen they became brides. Chuza was likely an older man with a strong prior résumé in management that got him his post as the king's finance minister. Some scholars suggest that he had died by the time Joanna, in need of healing, approached Jesus. Then, as an independently wealthy widow, she could leave the palace and join the itinerant band of disciples following Jesus and caring for his physical needs.

We know that she had the freedom to travel with Jesus down to Jerusalem for each of the great national feasts. On their final trip, she was there when he was arrested, tried, condemned, and crucified. She and the other women in the band were there at the cross as they watched Jesus die. They followed Nicodemus and Joseph of Arimathea to the tomb in which Jesus's body was laid. They were first at the tomb on Easter morning with spices to anoint Jesus's body properly. And they were the first to hear the angelic announcement: "He is risen just as he had promised!" She was among those who were the first to take resurrection news to the terrified disciples in hiding (Luke 24:10). Then, after Jesus's ascension to the Father, she was likely one of the women with Mary, the mother of Jesus, in that upper room prayer meeting (Acts 1:14).

Then came that life-changing moment when "on the day of Pentecost all the believers were meeting together in one place. Suddenly there was a sound from heaven like the roaring of a mighty windstorm, and it filled the house where they were sitting. Then what looked like flames or tongues of fire appeared and settled on each of them. And everyone present was filled with the Holy Spirit" (Acts 2:1–4). As one of the believers, Joanna was no doubt in that group. Imagine how she must have felt later in the day when she heard the apostle Peter quote the Old Testament prophet Joel:

"In the last days," God says, "I will pour out my Spirit upon all people. Your sons and daughters will prophesy. . . . In those days I will pour out my Spirit even on my servants—men and women alike—and they will prophesy." (Acts 2:17–18)

If the prophecy had indeed been realized as Peter had declared, then a new day had dawned: men and women alike would proclaim the truth of God.

Andronicus and Junia in Rome

Back to our mystery pair. How did Paul describe them? What were those clues given in Paul's letter?

1. Their names were given (Andronicus and Junia).
2. They were Jews.
3. They had been in prison with the apostle Paul.
4. They were highly respected among the apostles.
5. They became followers of Christ before Paul was converted.
6. They had "seen Jesus" during his earthly ministry.

We checked off the first clue when we learned that Junia is the Roman or Latin equivalent of the Hebrew name Joanna. Now we can also check off the second clue: Joanna/Junia was a Jew from Galilee. We can't check off clues 3 and 4 because we don't have that information. But we can check off clues 5 and 6 because we know that Joanna/Junia was part of Jesus's band of followers during his earthly ministry—she had "seen Jesus."

Now consider Joanna's credentials for ministry and apostleship. She was Jewish and spoke Hebrew or Aramaic. She had lived in a Roman palace in a Roman city and had probably been given a Roman name as part of her identification. It's likely that she also spoke Latin. She knew how to move in Roman circles.

But when we come to the name Andronicus, we're thrown back by the fact that Joanna was married to Chuza. Chuza was not a Jew; he was a Nabatean. In no way could he morph into Andronicus. But if we recall that he was already an older man when Joanna married him at a young age, and also that life expectancies in the first century were relatively brief, it's not unreasonable to assume that he most likely had died. Joanna would have been a widow, no longer attached to the Roman palace, but free to travel with the Jesus band as one of its benefactors.

Now as Junia, she's living in Rome. How could she have gotten from Galilee to Rome? Here is a potential clue. In his first letter to the churches in Asia Minor, Peter closes with this enigmatic statement, "Your sister church here in Babylon sends you greetings" (1 Peter 5:13). "Babylon" was a way of referring to Rome without mentioning the city by name. All first-century sources are agreed that while God had sent Paul to the Gentiles of Turkey and Greece, God had sent Peter as the apostle to the citadel of Roman power, Rome itself. But we still have not solved the question of how Junia got to Rome, or how Andronicus enters the picture.

Scholars point to the way in which corresponding Hebrew and Roman names had a certain similarity in spelling or sound. For example, we can see it in the shared letters between "Joanna" and "Junia." And between the rhyming of "Paul" and "Saul." It's possible that Andronicus was the Roman form of Andrew. Had the widowed Joanna at some point married Andrew, the brother of Peter and one of the Twelve? On the one hand, that's just a fanciful idea we cannot prove or disprove. On the other hand, it would have made sense for Peter to take his brother and his Latin-speaking sister-in-law along with him on his long journey to the heart of the Roman Empire. Junia's early years in the Roman palace in Tiberias would have provided amazing preparation for later missionary work in Rome.

Does making a connection between Andrew and Andronicus measure up to the clues we have? Andrew was a Jew. He was one of the earliest followers of Jesus (Matthew 10:1–4). He clearly meets clues 1, 2, 5, and 6. Because Andrew and Joanna both traveled with Jesus during his earthly ministry, we can assume that they knew one another. But whether they married one another is pure speculation. We also don't know whether he and Joanna/Junia were in prison with the apostle Paul at some point. Nor do we have a clear statement in Scripture that this pair was highly esteemed among the apostles. We only know that Andrew, with his brother Peter, was one of the first named apostles.

Although we aren't able to put together all of the pieces of Paul's puzzle, there are enough pieces in place to help us see that Joanna is the leading candidate for Junia, an apostle in Rome. As you recall what you've learned of her life story, can you see how God's Spirit was at work years earlier in preparing a young Jewish bride in Galilee for her ministry as an apostle to the Romans? Or how God's Spirit used Joanna's illness to put her in touch with Jesus? Or how those years as part of Jesus's band gave her ongoing access to the teachings of our Lord that would be foundational in all future ministry? God's Spirit used every part of her exposure to Jesus in his earthly ministry—the miracles, the teachings, the modeling of that upside-down Kingdom—to prepare her to teach others accurately and clearly the way to a relationship with God. She was then sent to Rome to teach others what Jesus had taught her.

It's highly unlikely that Joanna as a teenage bride could have imagined the way God would one day use every bit of her experience in a Roman palace. It's often the same for us. Can you look back on your earlier years and see things that didn't seem important at the time, but later God used to change your life? It's in the rearview mirror of life that we sometimes can get the best glimpses of God's strategic working in our lives. The mystery of some of our old experiences can be solved when we realize how intimately God has been at work in us.

God's Spirit is always at work in our lives. Sometimes it's the painful experiences that cause us to move in a different direction in life. Other times it's a preparation we hadn't valued as it was happening, but which turns out to prepare us for the next thing God puts into our hands to do for his Kingdom. Trust God's Spirit to lead you. Whether you recognize it or not, God is already at work in your life.

• • •

QUESTIONS FOR PERSONAL REFLECTION OR GROUP DISCUSSION

1. The chapter explores the available clues to solve the puzzle of Junia's identity and her qualifications for the ministry of apostleship. In what ways, if any, has your own personal or spiritual journey been a puzzle to you? What "clues" or missing pieces have you discovered that help you understand more about your identity, your purpose, or the gifts God has given you for ministry?

2. What little we can piece together about Joanna's life nevertheless reveals many ups and downs—from an aristocratic upbringing and life in a Roman palace, to possible young widowhood and a debilitating illness. And yet all of these experiences not only led her to meet Jesus and receive healing, but also prepared her for a ministry of apostleship. As you reflect on your own life, how would you describe your ministry "preparation"— the ups and downs that have equipped you, or are equipping you now, to love others in Jesus's name?

9

Mary, Tryphena, Tryphosa, Persis, Lois, and Eunice
God's Spirit Guides Us in Different Paths

What does it take to get your name in the news? It seems that you have to have accomplished something great or to have done something very bad. Most of us are happy to live our quiet lives without having to see our names splashed across news headlines. Why? Because we haven't accomplished anything we'd consider a great feat, and we want to make sure we aren't newsworthy for having done a terrible deed. In God's upside-down Kingdom, however, your life might be more newsworthy than you realize.

The women who were newsworthy in the New Testament letters were often those we might easily overlook today. They included women who were "hard workers" (nature of that work unspecified) or were homebodies, tucked away in a corner but busy building faith and God's Word into a child.

Scattered in various letters written by the apostle Paul are the names of six such newsworthy women, each of whom was recognized and honored within the early Christian communities. How do we know this? Simple: because we have their names. The renowned biblical scholar Richard Bauckham reminds us that the people whose names appear in New Testament letters are those who distinguished themselves as outstanding ministry workers or were well-known among the churches for other reasons. These would include the women we've already met in this book, such as Dorcas, Lydia, Damaris, Priscilla, Phoebe, and Joanna/Junia. But now we turn to six additional newsworthy women, some of whom might otherwise be easily overlooked.

HARD WORKERS IN THE LORD

As we continue reading through Paul's greetings to various Roman Christians at the end of his long letter, we come to four names that we may find unfamiliar:

> Greet Mary, who worked very hard for you. (ROMANS 16:6 NIV)

> Greet Tryphena and Tryphosa, those women who work hard in the Lord. Greet my dear friend Persis, another woman who has worked very hard in the Lord. (ROMANS 16:12 NIV)

What did these women have in common? They were "hard workers," all of them.

When you think of people who are hard workers, what characteristics come to mind? What words would you use to describe them? Diligent? Committed? Persevering? Single-minded? Undeterred? Another good word we could use to describe hard workers is *stalwart*—such folks are resolute and determined, unfaltering in their commitments regardless of the pain, cost, or inconvenience required. They are dependable and faithful. Whether their commitment is to the care of a sick friend or relative, to earning a living in a difficult workplace, or to some seemingly menial task at church, the hard workers will get the job done without fanfare or expectations of praise or reward. We know we can count on them.

However, as admirable as these traits are, does such committed diligence really merit being called newsworthy? Well, yes. On television's nightly news broadcasts, the newsworthy "hero" usually just did what had to be done, but in a risky situation. So perhaps the fact of risk is what makes someone's action newsworthy. Seen in that light, part of what makes Mary, Tryphena, Tryphosa, and Persis notable is not just that they worked hard, but that their hard work was "in the Lord."

As you read that, did you scratch your head, wondering how doing their work "in the Lord" made that a newsworthy risk? Perhaps one factor that we easily forget but was front and center in the lives of first-century Christians was the unpredictable persecutions that all followers of Jesus Christ had to live with constantly. All Jewish Christians in Rome were expelled for several years by the Emperor Claudius. Then, during the years that Nero reigned in Rome, he thought nothing of using Christians as human torches to light his gardens at night. And who can forget the "games" in the Coliseum in which Christians were pitted against hungry wild animals? Hard work "in the Lord" (or "for the Lord," as some translations put it) was work for a cause that often carried a Danger sign attached.

In spite of the intermittent dangers, these four women continuously poured all of their energy and creativity into God's work for Christ and his Kingdom. Their notability wasn't for some civic position or task. They concentrated all of their efforts on the work of building up the body of Christ in Rome, whatever the danger.

But there is additional significance to the fact of their hard work. It lies in how these women went about their work. They were hard workers *in the Lord*. They worked in the strength of the Lord, their God. That may sound promising but nebulous: what did it really mean for these hard workers? At the very least, it includes three implications that are as true for us today as they were for those first-century, hard-working women.

IMPLICATION 1: **Hard workers in the Lord are realistic about the limits of their own strength.** We may think that the very term "hard worker" means a relentless worker, someone who never takes a break. But we need to heed the ancient maxim, "Know thyself." Staying with a hard task requires that we are realistic about both our strengths and our limits. If we don't acknowledge our limits, we won't be able to assess realistically what we can or cannot attempt.

Have you ever taken on tasks or opportunities that taxed you—and those around you—beyond your ability to cope? Did you feel reluctant to say no to others' requests, or feel guilty when you did? Or have you agreed to host an elaborate celebratory dinner when your available time and resources were already stretched too thin? Or in an effort to please the boss or a customer, perhaps you've committed to a work deliverable that no one could accomplish within the given timeframe. If you can relate to any of these scenarios, then you know the consequences of failing to be realistic about your strengths and your limits. In the end, you feel like the worst rather than the best version of yourself, and you have little to offer others. And trust me, you're not alone in this—we've pretty much all been there!

If we want to be hard workers in the Lord who are in Kingdom work for the long haul, we must be realistic about our limitations. Not only is there no shame in weakness and limits, there is no divine strength available to us without them. Hard workers in the Lord do best to begin by acknowledging the limits of their own strength.

IMPLICATION 2: **Hard workers in the Lord are realistic about the world.** Just as hard workers are realistic about themselves, they are also realistic about the world in which they work. They know that this world is "no friend of grace." The apostle Paul put it even more bluntly at the end of his letter to the Christians in Ephesus:

> Be strong in the Lord and in his mighty power. . . . For we are not fighting against flesh-and-blood enemies, but against evil rulers and authorities of the unseen world, against mighty powers in this dark world, and against evil spirits in the heavenly places. (EPHESIANS 6:10, 12)

The apostle John weighed in when he ended his first letter with this reminder: "We know that . . . the world around us is under the control of the evil one" (1 John 5:19). Those first-century women would need no reminder of that reality. We, on the other hand, may not recognize as clearly as they did the cosmic battle being fought between the kingdoms of this world and the Kingdom of our God. Our relative safety and security may blind us to this cosmic reality. If that is our case, we may miss the necessity of the third implication.

IMPLICATION 3: **Hard workers in the Lord rely on God's Spirit for strength and wisdom.** Given the first two implications—that we recognize our human limitations and that we acknowledge the powers of evil in the world—we must rely on God's promise to be with us and to empower us. Jesus made that promise as his final word in Matthew's gospel: "Be sure of this: I am with you always, even to the end of the age" (Matthew 28:20). As we each go about our daily tasks or as we minister to others through the church or in our community, we are never alone. Jesus told his followers that when he returned to the Father, he would send the Holy Spirit who would be our guide (John 16:13). God's Spirit is with us to lead us into truth. This includes the truth about ourselves, the truth about our world, and the truth about God's strengthening presence in our lives.

However, when we acknowledge our limits—and live and serve others within those limits—we discover a wonderful paradox. The apostle Paul described it this way: "When I am weak, then I am strong" (2 Corinthians 12:10). How so? When he was tormented by some undisclosed "thorn in the flesh" and three times begged God to remove it, God's answer was "My power works best in weakness" (12:9). If we want to be steady and stalwart in our work for God, we'll live into the reality that our "help comes from the LORD" (Psalm 121:2). In God's upside-down Kingdom, that's the formula for sustaining hard workers.

WHAT WAS THE HARD WORK OF THESE FOUR WOMEN?

Paul called Mary, Tryphena, Tryphosa, and Persis "hard workers in the Lord" (*polla ekopiasen en kurio*). What exactly were they hard at work doing? We don't know the specifics. We do know, however, that Paul also used the same Greek phrase to describe his own ministry:

> We *work wearily* [*kopiomen*] with our own hands to earn our living. (1 CORINTHIANS 4:12, emphasis added)

> Perhaps all my *hard work* [*kekopiaka*] with you was for nothing. (GALATIANS 4:11, emphasis added)

> On the day of Christ's return, I will be proud that . . . my *work was not useless* [*ekopiase*]. (PHILIPPIANS 2:16, emphasis added)

Were these women in Rome doing what Paul was doing elsewhere? Were they perhaps outside Rome itinerating in other Italian towns, preaching the Good News? Were they starting new house churches in Rome itself? We don't know the answers to those questions beyond Paul's use of the term for both himself and for these women. However, we do have one piece of information that sheds some light on how highly Paul esteemed those who were hard workers in the Lord. In referring to a family who "are spending their lives in service to God's people," Paul told the Christians in Corinth to "submit to them and others like them who serve with such devotion [*sunergounti kai kopionti*]" (1 Corinthians 16:16). Whatever the nature of the ministry of these four women, their service not only made them worthy of honor, but also earned them spiritual authority. According to Paul, the proper response to those who serve with devotion—who give their lives in service—is to follow their lead, to "submit to them."

Elsewhere in his letters, the apostle Paul talks about the single-mindedness athletes bring to their training:

> All athletes are disciplined in their training. They do it to win a prize that will fade away, but we do it for an eternal prize. So I run with purpose in every step. (1 CORINTHIANS 9:25–26)

That may well describe these remarkable women whom Paul singled out as hard workers in the Lord.

In a world in which many Christians sit back and let others carry forward the work for Christ and his Kingdom, those who are diligent, committed hard workers for Jesus are genuinely newsworthy. These are women who persevered in their commitments to Jesus without looking back. They refused to quit. They were newsworthy indeed.

God's Spirit leads some women into up-front ministries that others can see. To this point in our study, we've looked at women active in some kind of ministry—ministries of care, like Dorcas's concern for the poor and for widows; ministries of benefaction, like Joanna's and Lydia's; ministries to intellectuals, like Damaris's; church leaders, like deacon Phoebe; apostles, like Junia; or coworkers of Paul, like Priscilla. Then there are the four women Paul singled out as hard workers. But all of these women constitute only one part of the picture of notable women in the New Testament churches.

LOIS AND EUNICE: A MOTHER AND DAUGHTER OF UNFEIGNED FAITH

We now meet another kind of hard worker recorded on the pages of the New Testament. These are the first-century hard workers whose Kingdom task was their commitment to the vital ministry of godly parenting. They were essential to God's work in their own time, and today their "daughters" are equally vital to God's work. Anyone who thinks that parenting a child well is not "hard work" hasn't undertaken that task!

Godly parenting may not be as publicly newsworthy as the hard work in ministry of Tryphena or Tryphosa or Mary or Persis. But God sees the worth of such mothers' labor, and crowns them with a blessing: *Well done, my daughter. You have been faithful over the years in training your children in godliness. Rest now in the knowledge that heaven sees and applauds your labor. The time will come when your children rise up and call you blessed* (Proverbs 31:28).

In the town of Lystra in central Turkey, a mother named Eunice and a grandmother named Lois instilled faith and the truth of God's Word into their young son and grandson named Timothy. Little did they know how important their faithful work would be to an entire church several decades later. To appreciate their accomplishment, we need to know the backstory that ultimately enabled Timothy to play a pivotal role in rescuing a fragmented first-century church from the grip of heresy.

The apostle Paul, with his coworkers Priscilla and Aquila, had spent three difficult years starting house churches across the important city of Ephesus in the southwestern corner of Turkey. Unquestionably, Ephesus had been the apostle's most challenging assignment: it was the only city in which both Jews and Gentiles had opposed him (Acts 19:8–9, 23–31). It was also at Ephesus that Paul had fought with wild beasts and had come under such pressure that he even despaired for his life (1 Corinthians 15:32).

Years later, on his way back to Jerusalem at the end of his third missionary journey, Paul met with the Ephesian elders in Miletus, the seaport for inland Ephesus. There, he reminded the elders that starting those churches in Ephesus had been done "with many tears" (Acts 20:19, 31). And then he warned that there were more tears to come. God's Spirit had revealed to him that a spiritual disaster was threatening the Ephesian churches:

> I know that false teachers, like vicious wolves, will come among you after I leave, not sparing the flock. Even some men from your own group will rise up and distort the truth in order to draw a following. Watch out! (ACTS 20:29–31)

Paul didn't mince words. In no uncertain terms, he urged the elders to be alert and head off what was coming.

Unfortunately, the elders either failed to heed Paul's warning or their efforts were too little too late. Several years later, as Paul sat chained in a Roman prison, the predicted disaster had happened. The congregations in Ephesus were reeling from both internal and external assaults, heretical teachings upending the congregations. But in spite of the devastation, Paul believed the churches were still salvageable (1 Timothy 1:3). To step in from the outside and clean up the mess, Paul sent his young coworker Timothy back to Ephesus.

Field-Testing Timothy's Training

What kind of leader would it take to deal with such a complex, multifaceted disaster? What do we know about the kind of person Timothy was? It's in Paul's second letter to Timothy that we discover the makings of this young man. It came in two parts: a genuine faith in God (2 Timothy 1:5) and a solid grounding in Scripture (2 Timothy 3:14–17).

We hear about Timothy's faith when Paul says of him, "I remember your genuine faith, for you share the faith that first filled your grandmother Lois and your mother, Eunice. And I know the same faith continues strong in you" (2 Timothy 1:5). Timothy had a heritage of genuine faith from his grandmother and mother.

An older Bible translation describes these women's faith as "unfeigned." To feign something is to pretend or to be insincere. A feigned faith would be a sham faith, a faith that was merely for show and had no substance. It was not the kind of faith that could withstand the opposition Timothy would face in Ephesus. This dire situation called for genuine faith, a wholehearted, bedrock confidence that God would be at work in and through him. It did not, however, require what we might call a blind faith—a kind of magical thinking that God would somehow just work it all out. Before continuing with Timothy's backstory, it's important to make this distinction, because it's at this point that Christians today sometimes falter—not because they don't have a genuine faith, but because they misunderstand the nature of faith.

When I was in my late teens, I read this statement about faith in my King James Bible: "Now faith is the substance of things hoped for, the evidence of things not seen" (Hebrews 11:1). Somehow in my mind, I took that statement to mean that faith was the same thing as *certitude*. In other words, if I had faith, I would be absolutely certain about things.

Wrong.

Having a bedrock confidence in God is not the same thing as having an absolute certitude about how things will turn out. I may well move forward in faith because I am confident that God is with me, but that doesn't mean that I can be certain of outcomes. The Old Testament prophet Isaiah reminds us that God's ways are not our ways:

> "My thoughts are nothing like your thoughts," says the LORD, "and my ways are far beyond anything you could imagine. For just as the heavens are higher than the earth, so my ways are higher than your ways and my thoughts higher than your thoughts." (ISAIAH 55:8–9)

As I grew and learned more about the nature of faith, I discovered that faith and doubt are two sides of the same coin. Everything depends on whether I opt for "heads" or "tails." Do I choose to live on the faith-side of the coin (believing that God is good and will ultimately do only what is good)? Or do I choose to live on the doubt-side of the coin (believing that God's goodness is not guaranteed and he might let me down)? An older Christian once said, "Faith is stepping into the void and finding solid ground beneath." The faith-side of the coin is what enables me to step into the void, trusting God for the solid ground of the result. That kind of faith is grounded not in what I hope the outcome of any situation might be, but in what I know to be true from Scripture about who God is. Author and pastor

Dallas Willard puts it well when he writes, "We can never understand the life of faith seen in scripture and in serious Christian living unless we drop the idea of faith as a 'blind leap' and understand that faith is commitment to action, often beyond our natural abilities, *based upon the knowledge of God and God's ways.*"[1] When my decisions come from genuine faith, I can step into the unknown and the uncertain because God's unfailing love enfolds me and I can trust his work in my life.

Circumstances change but God's character does not. Faith leads me to choose to live and work out of that knowledge. And this takes us back to the reason why Timothy was the right person for the difficult task ahead of him in Ephesus. Although he was stepping into the unknown and the uncertain, his faith was genuine—he knew he could trust God for the outcome, whatever it might be.

But Timothy also had a second gift from his mother and grandmother that he could rely on: it was his knowledge of God's Word. Lois and Eunice had thoroughly grounded Timothy in the Scriptures. Paul spelled out how that grounding would anchor Timothy when assailed by the fierce winds of heresy in Ephesus:

> You must remain faithful to the things you have been taught. You know they are true, for you know you can trust those who taught you. You have been taught the holy Scriptures from childhood, and they have given you the wisdom to receive the salvation that comes by trusting in Christ Jesus. All Scripture is inspired by God and is useful to teach us what is true and to make us realize what is wrong in our lives. It corrects us when we are wrong

and teaches us to do what is right. God uses it to prepare and equip his people to do every good work. (2 TIMOTHY 3:14–17)

Not only did Timothy share the genuine faith modeled by his grandmother and mother, but Lois and Eunice also took him, step by step, through the Scriptures as an anchor for his life. In Ephesus, Timothy would need to combat all kinds of heresies and the difficult people promoting them. How could he restore order, establish what was true, and bring these people back to the truth? It was that early and continuous training in God's Word that gave him a basis not only for discerning and correcting heresy, but also for dealing with difficult people. Paul could trust Timothy with this difficult assignment because he knew Timothy's faith was genuine and that he had a solid formation in Scripture.

Do you see how God's Spirit leads, sometimes building a solid foundation under us for something in the distant future that we can't even imagine? Lois and Eunice, in the years of Timothy's childhood, could not have imagined that the day would come when he would draw upon every part of that foundation to rescue the Ephesians from their entanglement in heresy. It is the same for us. We may not have seen the point of much that we learned or experienced years earlier, but as adults we take that backward glance in the rearview mirror of life, and we then can say, "Aha, so that's what all that training was about so long ago." At that moment we sense that surge of gratitude coursing through us as we recognize the gift we were given years before we knew we needed it.

How Did Lois and Eunice Come to This Faith?

How did Lois and Eunice come by the faith they then passed on to Timothy? For the answer, let's shift back in time to explore their backstory. It began with Paul's first missionary journey in the south-central part of Turkey. In Acts 14, he and Barnabas were in the town of Lystra. As Paul preached, he noticed a man lame from birth. Somehow, God's Spirit alerted Paul that the man had faith to be healed. So when Paul called in a loud voice, "Stand up!" the man did so and began walking around. A miracle! How could this be?

Astonished, the folks in Lystra decided that these visitors must be some of the Greek gods come to earth! Because Paul was the speaker, they determined he must be the god Hermes and Barnabas must be Zeus. Because the temple of Zeus was on the outskirts of the town, the temple priest and town folk "brought bulls and wreaths of flowers to the town gates, and they prepared to offer sacrifices to the apostles" (Acts 14:13). Paul and Barnabas were dismayed and did their best to convince the people that they were mere mortals. Even so, they "could scarcely restrain the people from sacrificing to them" (Acts 14:18). (You can read the whole fascinating story in Acts 14:8–20.)

As Paul continued to preach the gospel of God's love and grace through Jesus Christ, it's possible that in the audience that day were two Jewish women, Lois and Eunice, perhaps with little Timothy by their side. This may have been the moment when they became believers in Jesus Christ as God's Messiah. Integrating their knowledge of the Hebrew Scriptures with their newfound faith in Christ, these women then carefully trained young Timothy in genuine faith and the knowledge of God's truth in Scripture.

Years later, when Paul, now traveling with Silas, returned to Lystra on his second missionary journey, he was so impressed with young Timothy that he asked him to join them in their work. Thus began a long ministry partnership that took Timothy to places he likely never dreamed he'd see and gave him experiences he may not otherwise have chosen but was well suited to engage.

We first met Timothy as part of Lydia's story (chapter 4). With Paul and Silas, he had crossed from Turkey into northern Greece. We noted then that Timothy, the son of a Greek father, would be especially helpful to the apostles in this new territory. As he traveled with Paul and Silas first to Philippi, then to Thessalonica, then Berea, then south to Athens and Corinth, the young man matured quickly, so much so that when Paul needed a trusted colleague to send to Ephesus in later years, Timothy was ready.

Paul recognized, however, that some Ephesians might consider Timothy's relative youth a handicap. How could he effectively deal with those older men and women who were spreading heresy in the Ephesian churches? Knowing ahead of time this might be a problem, Paul gave Timothy some advance coaching:

> Don't let anyone think less of you because you are young. Be an example to all believers in what you say, in the way you live, in your love, your faith, and your purity. (1 TIMOTHY 4:12)

Note how Timothy was to deal with that handicap: he would win by living out an example of love, faith, and purity in both word and deed. That's a good formula for any Christian facing criticism from any source. Regardless of the outcome, when what we say and how we live are guided by demonstrations of our love, our faith, and our purity, we win.

MINISTRY CAN TAKE MANY FORMS

Four of the women we've discussed had the opportunity to become hard workers in the Lord with the apostle Paul. They spent their lives in public service to God's people, and we know their names more than two thousand years later because of their noteworthy devotion. Two other women distinguished themselves behind the scenes by becoming models of genuine faith and teachers of God's Word to a child. Who could have predicted that grandmother Lois and mother Eunice would prepare a young boy in faith and in the Scriptures in such a way that he would be able to take on one of the most difficult apostolic tasks dealing with multiple forms of heresy in Ephesus?

God had given Eunice and her husband a son, Timothy. She and her mother took seriously the responsibility of training that little boy in faith and in the Scriptures. But children grow up and move away, helping us realize that there are seasons in our lives. We don't know in what ways Eunice and Lois may have later become involved in the church ministries in Lystra, once their responsibility for Timothy had ended. Nor do we know whether at an earlier time in their lives Tryphena, Tryphosa, Mary, or Persis may have spent time quietly training a child in God's truth. In every case, God's Spirit was at work, leading each woman to the ministry she was to engage, whether in the home or out working hard with God's apostle. And when one task was completed, God's Spirit was there, ready to lead willing women on to the next ministry.

Sometimes we're more impressed with the obvious exploits of those who go to distant lands under dangerous conditions than with the quiet, steadfast work of women rearing their children in genuine faith and in the knowledge of God's Word. But both kinds of ministry are necessary. As we see in the lives of these six women, the particular ministry God calls us to, whether public or behind the scenes, isn't what matters most. What does matter is that we work hard at whatever God places in our hand to do, that we pursue it with a genuine faith, and that we are grounded in the truth of the Scriptures.

Inheritances, whether monetary or spiritual, are passed down from generation to generation. Timothy's grandmother, Lois, and his mother, Eunice, modeled a genuine faith in God. The Proverbs note that "Good people leave an inheritance to their grandchildren" (Proverbs 13:22). Timothy received a glorious inheritance from grandmother Lois and mother Eunice—not a temporal inheritance, but an enduring inheritance of genuine faith and a knowledge of God's Word. Theirs may turn out to be the most valuable ministry of all.

• • •

QUESTIONS FOR PERSONAL REFLECTION OR GROUP DISCUSSION

1. Who has been a model for you of a "hard worker in the Lord"? In what ways did/do their words and actions reflect the three implications that must be true of hard workers in the Lord (pages 146–148)?

2. Based on your personal experience or your observations of others, what distinctions, if any, would you make between being a "hard worker" and being a "hard worker in the Lord"? Share any personal examples that come to mind to illustrate your response.

3. Based on what the apostle Paul noted and esteemed about six women, this chapter explored what constitutes "newsworthy" ministry, some of which was public and some of which took place behind the scenes. How would you characterize the esteem given to various forms of ministry within your own Christian community? What tends to be routinely recognized and affirmed? What, if anything, tends to be overlooked?

4. What kind of faith inheritance do you most want to leave for those who will come after you?

10

Euodia and Syntyche

God's Spirit Guides Us to See Ourselves as God's Servants

I was something of a tomboy as a kid. There were no girls my age on our block and my brother had lots of friends who let me play softball or touch football with them. I took pride in being able to knock that softball over the corner billboard. One fall day, however, when we were playing touch football, I had the ball, was face-down on the grass on top of it, and the guys were piling on top of me. The next thing I knew, an elderly neighbor was shouting and pulling those boys away. Then he stood me up and sent me home, telling me that girls should *never* play touch football. That ended my tomboy days. I was a girl. I shouldn't play football. End of discussion. And it was far from the last time I would be told that there were things I simply could not or should not do because I am female.

Sadly, one of the things I and other women have sometimes been told we cannot do is to hold a leadership position within the church. However, as we have explored throughout this book, women like Priscilla, Phoebe, Junia, Mary, Tryphena, Tryphosa, Persis, and others in first-century churches performed the same kinds of ministries as their male counterparts. In so doing, were they "leaders"? When we read secular leadership books, we know what the word means in the business world. But does the word carry the same meaning once we bring it inside a church building? This leads us to two questions: 1) What do we mean when we use the word "leadership" in Christian ministry? 2) How does a biblical understanding of leadership affect how we work together in ministry?

QUESTION 1: WHAT DO WE MEAN WHEN WE USE THE WORD "LEADERSHIP" IN CHRISTIAN MINISTRY?

Before tackling that question directly, we need to see the broader context of leadership: how would most people define the word *leadership*? We know that competing meanings dominate businesses and governments, and sometimes spill into churches. So what secular notions compete with a biblical understanding of leadership?

Management consultant and author Peter Drucker famously defined a leader as "anyone who has followers." But that general definition won't take us very far. If we look to the business world, most books on leadership would define a leader as the person in a top position—the CEO, the CFO, or the COO. We're then told that this person's role in business is to cast a vision for an organization that others are expected to follow.

But in many business settings, not every person at the top is responsible for casting a vision. This is where some leadership gurus distinguish between *managers* and *leaders*. Leaders are those who cast the vision, and managers are those who implement it at all levels. But in both cases, whether a manager or a leader, that person is over others in a way that demands a "following"—someone has to carry out that vision. So leadership in a business context has multiple expressions.

But what about in other settings? For example, in the military, leadership is not about vision or even management. It's about who is in command—who has the authority to tell the troops where to go, what to do, and when to do it. Is that management or is it leadership? Hmm. If we look at the animal kingdom, the "leader" is the creature who is the biggest, fastest, most beautiful, or most assertive. In nature, leadership is defined by dominance. Consider just one more example—horse racing. In a race, the leader is simply the one who is out in front, ahead of the pack. The jockey on the lead horse isn't leading anyone else; he or she is simply striving to be first to reach a mutually desired goal.[1]

Clearly, the context in which we consider what a leader is matters. What may be true in a business is certainly not true in a zoo. So are we talking about a business, an army, a zoo, or a horse race? Our definition changes as the context changes. That fact matters a great deal when we talk about leadership in the church.

When we return to some books on leadership, most of them tell us that a leader is defined by two common denominators: that person must have both a *position* and *power*. Behind both of these lurks the issue of "authority"—who is in charge, who has the power. History books are packed with stories of those who have had positions with power. Historians seldom focus on those who have neither.

So much for some of the secular literature on leadership. We turn our attention now to what Jesus taught about leadership, which is how we will get our answer to the question: What do we mean when we use the word "leadership" in Christian ministry?

Do you recall the incidents from Matthew 20 and John 13 that we looked at in chapter 7? They bear repeating here as we try to get our arms around the meaning of that word *leadership* in Christian ministry. When the mother of James and John asked Jesus to give her two sons positions of power at his right or left hand in the coming Kingdom, he decided it was time to give all twelve of the disciples some solid instruction on leadership:

> "You know that the rulers in this world lord it over their people, and officials flaunt their authority over those under them. But among you it will be different. Whoever wants to be a leader among you must be your servant, and whoever wants to be first among you must become your slave. For even the Son of Man came not to be served but to serve others and to give his life as a ransom for many." (MATTHEW 20:25–28)

Jesus begins by acknowledging how leadership is defined in the context of the world, where leaders are by definition those who flaunt their position and authority to the detriment of those under them. And then he makes a striking statement: "But among you it will be different." In other words, *Among you, leadership will reverse what it is in the world.* And lest anyone think he is merely talking about making some minor tweaks to the world's model, Jesus goes on to describe precisely what he means by "different." Leaders in the world are rulers and officials; leaders in the Kingdom are servants and slaves. Leaders in the world flaunt their authority over others; leaders in the Kingdom give their lives away serving others. Leaders in the world are all the same; leaders in the Kingdom are different—radically so. We lead as we serve. Jesus is our model, and the Kingdom of God is our context.

So intent was Jesus on driving home this radical truth about leadership that one of the last things he did in his few remaining hours before his arrest and crucifixion was to make an object lesson out of it for the twelve disciples. This is how he demonstrated what Kingdom leadership looks like:

> So he got up from the table, took off his robe, wrapped a towel around his waist, and poured water into a basin. Then he began to wash the disciples' feet, drying them with the towel he had around him. . . . After washing their feet, he put on his robe again and sat down and asked, "Do you understand what I was doing? You call me 'Teacher' and 'Lord,' and you are right, because that's what I am. And since I, your Lord and Teacher, have washed your feet, you ought to wash each other's feet. I have given you an example to follow. Do as I have done to you. . . . Now that you know these things, God will bless you for doing them." (JOHN 13:4–5, 12–15, 17)

Again and again throughout the Gospels, Jesus turns the values and perspective of the world upside down. In leadership, as in every other area of the Christian life, Jesus reminds his followers, "Whoever wants to be a leader among you must be your servant, and whoever wants to be first among you must become your slave" (Matthew 20:26–27). Whether the context is an economic kingdom, a political kingdom, a cultural kingdom, or any other kind of kingdom people set up for themselves, life and leadership in God's Kingdom is radically *different*. It's nothing like the kingdoms of this world. So when we use the word "leadership" in Christian ministry, we mean taking Jesus's upside-down model for leadership so seriously that we accept our place as servant of all.

QUESTION 2: HOW DOES A BIBLICAL UNDERSTANDING OF LEADERSHIP AFFECT HOW WE WORK TOGETHER IN MINISTRY?

In the light of Jesus's powerful teaching about leadership, we need to evaluate how both men and women in the New Testament churches viewed and carried out leadership responsibilities. What motivated them? Was it that they were carrying out the ministry God's Spirit had put into their hands and hearts to do in a spirit of service? Or did any of them view ministry with an eye to power or position? It's always possible for even the best among us to be seduced by the siren call of power.

When we read Paul's letter to the Christians in Philippi, we are forced to pause when the apostle ruefully notes, "It's true that some [believers] are preaching out of jealousy and rivalry. But others preach about Christ with pure motives. . . . Those others do not have pure motives as they preach about Christ. They preach with selfish ambition, not sincerely" (Philippians 1:15, 17). Paul concludes that they're doing that to spite him as he sits silenced in prison.

Then, as we reach the final chapter of Paul's letter to the Philippian Christians, we read about two women leaders in the church who need help:

> Now I appeal to Euodia and Syntyche. Please, because you belong to the Lord, settle your disagreement. And I ask you, my true partner, to help these two women, for they worked hard with me in telling others the Good News. They worked along with Clement and the rest of my co-workers. (PHILIPPIANS 4:2–3)

What do we know about these two women? Paul calls them his coworkers as well as coworkers with Clement and Paul's other coworkers. They were evangelists, announcing the Good News of salvation in Jesus Christ.

Paul does *not* lump them in with those he named who were preaching out of jealousy and rivalry. But somehow something between them had erupted into public notice and needed to be dealt with. The New Living Translation calls it a "disagreement" between them, but other translations simply note that the two women had differing opinions about something important:

> "I plead with Euodia and I plead with Syntyche to be of the same mind in the Lord" (NIV).

> "I entreat Euodia and I entreat Syntyche to agree in the Lord" (ESV).

> "I urge Euodia and I urge Syntyche to live in harmony in the Lord" (NASB).

The literal translation of Paul's appeal in Greek is, "to think the same thing in the Lord."

Although we can't be certain that the women actually had a ministry-impeding disagreement, they clearly had differing opinions about something that somehow threatened the unity of the church. Disagreements can remain private, but when they spill over in public, they negatively impact others. If, in fact, the issue was a quarrel between these two leaders, it would make sense for the apostle Paul to bring in others to help these two women work through their issue.

According to Jesus, leadership in God's upside-down Kingdom is about seeing ourselves as servants, even as slaves, not as those "in authority." Whatever overturns that basic teaching disrupts God's work, such as those who preached out of jealousy to spite the apostle Paul. Or it could be leaders whose differing ideas collided in public in a disruptive way.

Whenever people work together, the possibility always lurks somewhere that they might disagree about something important. If a disagreement is settled quickly, the relationship between the parties and the work they do together can regain its momentum. But if the disagreement drags on and others get pushed into choosing sides, what had started out as a pleasant project quickly sours.

To deal with this, the apostle had already touched on the issue of handling disagreements earlier in his letter to the Philippians:

Make me truly happy by agreeing wholeheartedly with each other, loving one another, and working together with one mind and purpose. Don't be selfish; don't try to impress others. Be humble, thinking of others as better than yourselves. Don't look out only for your own interests, but take an interest in others too. You must have the same attitude that Christ Jesus had. (PHILIPPIANS 2:2–5)

Did Paul have Euodia and Syntyche in mind when he penned these words? Possibly. But as already noted, Paul also fingered others in Philippi who were preaching out of "selfish ambition rather than from pure motives." It wasn't only these two women in his sights. It was anyone whose motivation had been corrupted from service to selfish gain.

The antidote to such attitudes was the imperative statement: "You must have the same attitude that Christ Jesus had" (Philippians 2:5). We're called to follow Jesus's example of laying down his life for his friends (John 10:11). Why? Because it's the Kingdom version of leadership.

What was that attitude modeled by Jesus?

Though he was God, he did not think of equality with God as something to cling to. Instead, he gave up his divine privileges; he took the humble position of a slave and was born as a human being. When he appeared in human form, he humbled himself in obedience to God and died a criminal's death on a cross.

Therefore, God elevated him to the place of highest honor and gave him the name above all other names, that at the name of Jesus every knee should bow, in heaven and on earth and under the earth, and every tongue declare that Jesus Christ is Lord, to the glory of God the Father. (PHILIPPIANS 2:6–11)

It could be that ministering in the rough-and-tumble world of Roman Philippi may have caused Euodia and

Syntyche to lose sight of the pattern set by Jesus. We can't be sure what transpired between the two women, but we know that Paul appealed to them to think "the same thing in the Lord." He also reminded everyone in the Philippian church to follow the example of Jesus, who "gave up his divine privileges [and] took the humble position of a slave."

The Greek word translated as "slave," both here and in Jesus's statement that "whoever wants to be first among you must become your slave" (Matthew 20:27), is *doulos*, often translated "servant." The meaning is halfway between "slave" and "servant." Our notion of a slave is someone in bondage, placed there by someone else against his or her will. A *doulos* is not enslaved by someone else, but has voluntarily entered that position at the bottom of the social ladder. Jesus not only voluntarily placed himself in a position of servitude, but he calls us to do the same. The way to be "first" is to become "last," a slave. This is what leadership looks like in God's upside-down Kingdom.

HOW DOES THIS RELATE TO WOMEN IN LEADERSHIP?

Some have concluded that the problem was that Euodia and Syntyche could not get along in leadership, and that proves that women are not capable of leading and should not attempt it. But others see it in the light of 1 Timothy 2:12 (which we will discuss in chapter 12). In either case, behind most prohibitions of women in church leadership is the assumption that leadership is always a position of authority (despite Jesus's assertion that it is servanthood). Some of this has come from Bible translations that have inserted the notion of "office" into an understanding of the term. For example, the King James translation of Romans 11:13 is, "I magnify mine office." The word being translated as "office" is *diakonos*, meaning "service" or "ministry." Again, in Romans 12:4, the King James translation reads, "All members have not the same office." Once more, the word *office* is nowhere to be found in that text. But it was used to translate *praxis*, meaning "function." New Testament scholar Walter Liefeld reminds us that changing the sense of the biblical text to include the idea of an office implies a position with some kind of authority. But no such term exists in Christian literature before the time of Cyprian (circa AD 200–258). Liefeld concludes that while Jesus saw ministry as servanthood, some see it as "a power base giving an incumbent authority over the church." He wonders whether "one of the main reasons why many Christians feel uneasy about allowing women into the ministry is that they think this would give them power or authority that they think the Bible denies them."[2]

Once we adopt a notion of leadership as a position with authority, we've forsaken Jesus's clear statement that in God's Kingdom, we lead as we serve, from the bottom of the pile. It is just a step away from applying 1 Timothy 2:12 to women, then barring them from this secular notion of authority. That text reads "I do not let women teach men or have authority over them. Let them listen quietly." This is an important text and will be discussed in detail in chapter 12.

But our question here is whether biblical leadership is or is not a "position with authority." And when we listen to Jesus in Matthew 20:25, it's clearly servanthood, not the leadership of "the rulers in this world [who] lord it over their people and . . . flaunt their authority over those under them." The biblical question isn't who has authority over whom, but how all of us—men and women—are to serve together for God's glory.

It's significant that every time the apostle Paul talks about various ministries, it's always in the context of one's individual giftedness. Here is one example:

> In his grace, God has given us different gifts for doing certain things well. So if God has given you the ability to prophesy, speak out with as much faith as God has given you. If your gift is serving others, serve them well. If you are a teacher, teach well. If your gift is to encourage others, be encouraging. If it is giving, give generously. If God has given you leadership ability, take the responsibility seriously. And if you have a gift for showing kindness to others, do it gladly. (ROMANS 12:6–8)

When Paul penned those words, he didn't say that some of those gifts applied to men and others applied to women. The teaching was for all followers of Jesus Christ. Women as well as men have received a full spectrum of gifts meant to be used in ministry service. For women as well as for men, we lead when we use God's gifts in service to others. Our service is tied to the gifts God has given us. Ultimately, it's God's choice about the gifts we've been given. So we give thanks, we hone those gifts, and we use them as the servants of God that we are.

WE LEAD UNDER THE AUTHORITY OF JESUS

For some Christian women, the question of women in ministry leadership isn't a pressing one. They enjoy using such spiritual gifts as kindness, hospitality, service, or encouragement. However, for other women, particularly those with gifts of leadership or for teaching, this is a very pressing question indeed. But for all of us, regardless of the gifts we've been given, the bottom line is the example of our Savior, who gave up his divine privileges, took the position of a slave, humbled himself in obedience to God, and died a criminal's death on a cross. That's our model. It has nothing to do with positions of authority.

Because Jesus humbled himself, the apostle Paul reminds us that, "God elevated him to the place of highest honor and gave him the name above all other names, that at the name of Jesus every knee should bow, in heaven and on earth and under the earth, and every tongue declare that Jesus Christ is Lord, to the glory of God the Father" (Philippians 2:9–11). The one who died a criminal's death is now the King of Kings and Lord of Lords. In that light, Jesus's final words to his followers before his ascension to God in heaven were, "I have been given all authority in heaven and on earth. Therefore, go and make disciples. . . . And be sure of this: I am with you always, even to the end of the age" (Matthew 28:18–20).

This is our encouragement: Jesus has all the authority. We live and work under his authority. So we can confidently use our gifts wherever we are, knowing that we're never alone. Jesus is always with us. The one with authority is on our team, at our side, working in and through us. We can let that truth sink in and hold us as we go forth each day to serve in the power of our Lord Jesus Christ.

• • •

QUESTIONS FOR PERSONAL REFLECTION
OR GROUP DISCUSSION

1. As you were growing up, what messages did you receive from others or from your culture about what you could or could not do because you were female? For example, were certain activities, sports, or professions off limits? How did you respond to those messages, or what impact did they have on you?

2. The definition and understanding of what a leader is can change quite a bit from one context to the next (such as business, the military, the natural world, horse racing, etc.). What would you say is the primary context that has shaped your own understanding of what a leader is? What similarities and differences are there between the expectations that context places on leaders and the expectations Jesus placed on leaders?

3. What are your spiritual gifts? If leadership in God's upside-down Kingdom is about seeing ourselves as servants (rather than as those "in authority"), how would you describe what it might mean to be a leader by using your gifts?

11

Apphia and Philemon
God's Spirit Guides Us in a Blessed Alliance

Have you ever watched children's choices on a playground? Some head to swings or slides, equipment that they can enjoy by themselves. Others want to have fun on a teeter-totter. But what does it take for anyone to enjoy a teeter-totter? It's fun only if someone else is sitting on the opposite end of the board, and it helps if that other person is similar in size and weight. One thing is certain: you can't teeter-totter alone. Just as it takes two to tango, it takes two to teeter-totter.

The same principle holds true for marriage and for other relationships as well. Business analysts have found that because men and women think differently in some important ways, industrial boardrooms need both men and women interacting for the best solutions to any issues under discussion. One sex alone without the other sex will not grasp both the bigger picture and also the essential details that are part of that picture.

Throughout this book, most of the women we've looked at were singled out by Luke or Paul without any reference to a spouse, though we've met two couples working together—Priscilla and Aquila, and Andronicus and Junia. When we turn to Paul's short letter to Philemon, we meet another couple in the opening verses: Philemon and Apphia, who together host the church that meets in their house. Most scholars assume that Philemon and Apphia were husband and wife. In ways not detailed in the text, they worked together as leaders of the church in their home.

Is there any benefit gained from having men and women working together, leading a church? Support for that comes to us from several quarters. Of course, we begin with Genesis 1:26–28 in which God gave two tasks to the man and woman created in the divine image: to populate the earth and to serve as stewards of its resources. Added to that, however, is some fascinating new research about male and female brains that underscores the interdependence of men and women and why we need one another. Philemon needed Apphia, not just for help with tasks traditionally performed by women such as hospitality, but to bring the broader insights to their Kingdom work together that she was uniquely equipped physiologically to provide.

God's Plan Revealed in Creation

An important question Christians have wrestled with over the centuries has to do with how men and women are to relate to one another in the church and in the home. And yet we find that before we even knew to ask the question, God had embedded an answer into the very fabric of creation:

> Then God said, "Let us make human beings in our image, to be like us. They will reign over the fish in the sea, the

birds in the sky, the livestock, all the wild animals on the earth, and the small animals that scurry along the ground." So God created human beings in his own image. In the image of God he created them; male and female he created them. Then God blessed them and said, "Be fruitful and multiply. Fill the earth and govern it. Reign over the fish in the sea, the birds in the sky, and all the animals the scurry along the ground." (GENESIS 1:26–28)

God created humanity in two forms: male and female, man and woman. Both were created in the divine image and both received the same mandate: to fill the earth and to govern it. God didn't tell the woman to fill the earth and then tell the man to govern. He gave both commands to both the man and the woman.

It's easy to see how essential a man was to the "filling the earth" part: a woman could not conceive without him. But many of us have been taught that the governing part was meant to be done by the man alone. This perspective comes from Genesis 2, where we find God creating the woman and giving her a mandate of her own: "Then the LORD God said, 'It is not good for the man to be alone. I will make a helper who is just right for him'" (Genesis 2:18). So God gave the man a helper. On the basis of that verse, many Christians have since taught that the man should do most of the governing, but in a pinch when he needed help, the woman would be there to lend him a hand.

Note the translation of the biblical text: "I will make a helper who is just right for him." As we've seen in previous chapters, sometimes the choice of a word in a translation can mislead us, and in this case the word "helper" does just that. In our twenty-first-century thinking, a helper is a subordinate, like the apprentice who hands the plumber the right wrench. But when we look at the Hebrew word being translated as "helper," we need to back up and reconsider that notion.

The English word "helper" translates the Hebrew word *ezer*. *Ezer* is a fairly common word in the Old Testament, appearing twenty-one times. Two times it refers to the woman, Eve (here in Genesis 2:18 and again in 2:20). Three times *ezer* refers to strong nations or armies to which God's people appealed for help when threatened with extinction by Assyria or Babylon:

- The prophet Isaiah reminded Judah that relying on Egypt to help them against the enemy was a bad idea: "But by trusting Pharaoh, you will be humiliated . . . all who trust in him will be ashamed. He will not help [*ezer*] you. Instead, he will disgrace you" (Isaiah 30:3, 5). Egypt was not the help God's people needed.

- The prophet Daniel reminded the Jews that in a time of trouble to come, they would mistakenly rely on help that could not deliver them. "During these persecutions, little help [*ezer*] will arrive" (Daniel 11:34).

- The prophet Ezekiel detailed what would happen to Israel's leader, "the prince in Jerusalem," when the house of Israel would soon be sent into exile in Babylon: "I will scatter to every wind all who are around him, his helpers [*ezer*] and all his troops" (Ezekiel 12:14 NASB). God would make sure that "helpers" could not help this "rebellious house."

Thus we see that of the twenty-one times *ezer* is used in the Old Testament, it twice refers to Eve, and three times refers to strong forces God's people mistakenly rely on to save them when disaster is imminent. But what about the sixteen other times this word is used in the Bible?

In all of the sixteen remaining cases, *ezer* refers to God who is our "help."[1] And yet no one suggests that because God is our help that he is in any sense our subordinate. God is not subordinate to his creatures. When God created the woman as the man's *ezer*, he created someone who could bring help to the man, who was incomplete on his own. Scholars such as Philip Payne tell us that "*help* expresses that woman is a help/strength who rescues or saves man."[2]

This was God's plan in the beginning: together the man and the woman would fill the earth, and together they would govern it. Both were created in God's image, and both were charged with representing God's purposes for this new creation, Earth. They were created enough alike to be able to work together, and enough different so that they needed one another's unique strengths.

WHAT DIFFERENCE DOES BRAIN PHYSIOLOGY MAKE?

Until a few decades ago, information about the human brain was limited because researchers had to rely primarily on cadaver brains to learn about the structure and function of the human brain. Scientists had mapped the parts of the brain physically, but they could only speculate about how it actually functioned. For that, scientists needed tools that would allow them to watch living brains at work.

All of that changed with the invention of new technologies, such as fMRI, DTI, and PET scans.[3] If you google brain studies from any major research center (such as MIT,

Harvard, state universities, etc.), you'll quickly discover research demonstrating that male and female brains differ in surprising ways. While the differences are complex, they basically come down to the major differences between the left and right hemispheres of the brain and the consequent difference in the ways male and female brains use those hemispheres.

Noted British psychiatrist and brain scientist Iain McGilchrist tells us that while to the naked eye the hemispheres look alike, they are surprisingly different—physically and functionally.

Physically. The right hemisphere is longer, wider, and heavier than the left hemisphere. It has more neurons and more connective processes, permitting it to make more links more quickly between bits of data or information. If you look at pictures of the linking between the two hemispheres, you find that in the left hemisphere, the linking is primarily within the hemisphere, from front to back, whereas the right hemisphere provides stronger links between the two hemispheres. But the physical differences between the two hemispheres are not as significant as the functional differences.

Functionally. The left hemisphere is the detail side of the brain. It is characterized by narrowly focused attention. It gives priority to local communication. In contrast, the right hemisphere brings in the broad context, the global picture, or whatever is necessary for flexibility of thought. We turn to the left hemisphere when we need formulas for making things. At the same time, the left brain finds the right hemisphere's bigger picture distracting. While the left hemisphere takes the single solution that seems to fit best with what it already knows, the right hemisphere is always watching for discrepancies and looking for alternate solutions. In a sense, the two hemispheres are at cross-purposes with each other.

The right hemisphere integrates larger bodies of data and is constantly searching for patterns in things within their context. In contrast, the left hemisphere separates things *from* their context. In general, the tendency of the left hemisphere is to classify things into groups, whereas the tendency of the right hemisphere is to identify things individually. The left hemisphere has an affinity for what is mechanical, and its principal concern is usefulness. In contrast, the right hemisphere has an affinity for whatever is organic (in the sense of living matter) and its principal concern is social (for what concerns us as human beings). Because it is open to the interconnectedness of things, it plays an important role in our ability to put ourselves in someone else's context and empathize with that person. Can you see how empathy could get in the way of the left hemisphere's functioning? To optimize its work, the left hemisphere must screen out context, not bringing it in as the right hemisphere does.

McGilchrist is careful not to draw conclusions about the implications his research may suggest about differences between the brains of men and women, but other scientists have undertaken this work. When researchers at the Perelman School of Medicine (University of Pennsylvania) scanned the brains of more than four hundred men and more than five hundred women, they found pronounced differences between them. It turns out that in male brains, the neural connectivity moves from front to back within each hemisphere; in women's brains, there was more neural connectivity between the two hemispheres, which means that the broad band of nerve fibers called the *corpus callosum* that links the two hemispheres is thicker in female brains.

It also turns out that the back of the brain is where we perceive things, and the front of the brain is where we make sense of what we perceive, which then helps us determine how to act on it. So for any task (whether it's learning to ski or how to fix a defective appliance), if we have strong front-to-back connectivity, we're better able to accomplish our goal. At the same time, if we have more connections between the two hemispheres, we bring the big picture to the detail task in a way that may give us more options for a solution. The researchers tell us that with more links between hemispheres, women tend to be more adept at communicating, analyzing, and bringing intuition to their tasks. In short, their brains are physiologically predisposed to problem-solving in groups. As a result, women can keep several tasks going simultaneously in ways that men would find more challenging. Men tend to be better at learning and completing a single task at a time.

How men and women use language is also influenced by their differing brain physiology. While men primarily use the left hemisphere of the brain for language, women (who have more neural links between hemispheres) use both hemispheres for language. In general, it turns out that women think more inclusively or bilaterally than men. If you think back to the differences between the two brain hemispheres, you can see that the male brain is physiologically constructed to think more linearly, and the female brain to think more bilaterally or contextually.

Although all of these differences in male and female brains are physiological, we have tended to attach more value or weight to some ways of thinking rather than others—specifically, to the way male brains function. For example, to linear thinkers, contextual thinking doesn't always look like what they consider thinking. In reality, it's a complex form of thinking, but it has often been discredited by those who don't think in that way. It's not hard to see why such valuing of some kinds of thinking over others might create problems for women.

What Does This Have to Do with Men and Women Working Together in Ministry?

Let's go back to McGilchrist for a moment. As a philosopher as well as brain scientist, he looked at various historical eras and found that from the Enlightenment (1685–1815) onward, the intellectuals of the day concluded that only what we now refer to as left-brain activity was actual "thinking." What we now refer to as right-brain activity (such as using intuition) was not considered "thinking" at all. But if only left-brain activity is actual "thinking," there are consequences. McGilchrist writes:

> We could expect that there would be a loss of the broader picture, and a substitution of a more narrowly focused, restricted, but detailed, view of the world, making it perhaps difficult to maintain a coherent overview. . . . One would expect the left hemisphere to keep doing refining experiments on detail, at which it is exceedingly proficient, but to be correspondingly blind to what is not clear or certain, or cannot be brought into focus right in the middle of the visual field. In fact, one would expect a sort of dismissive attitude to anything outside of its limited focus,

because the right hemisphere's take on the whole picture would simply not be available to it.[4]

Think about that for a moment. It takes input from both the left and right hemispheres to get the full picture. It's not just that things would somehow be nicer if men and women pooled their thinking. Failing to do so narrows the scope of available input to the point that information essential to holistic decision-making is lost. McGilchrist's insight also gives some clarity to why some linear thinkers may be dismissive of anyone giving non-linear input.

Perhaps a simple illustration here would help. A couple decides to buy a new car. The left brains of both the man and the woman would be concerned with details about the car itself: engine type, gas mileage, trunk size. The right brains of both would be concerned with questions about how the car would be used: Could Aunt Margaret get in and out of this car easily when I take her to the grocery store each week? Is this car big enough to ferry the Brownie troop to an outing? However, given their different brain physiologies, the man is more likely to focus on the details about the car, and the woman more likely to focus on how the car would be used. For the left-brain thinker, the decision is about the car itself, without regard for other factors. But for the right-brain thinker, the decision is about the many ways the car must function in the family. There is no inherent value in one way of thinking over the other; they're just different, and both bring valuable information to bear on making a sound decision. In other words, considering the broad context for the car's use is just as important as considering gas mileage.

Men need women's perspectives and women need men's perspectives. God designed us to work together and to complement one another. While God sees both the details and the whole picture, men and women were created with different pieces of the puzzle that must be brought together to function well. Together, men and women form what author and scholar Carolyn Custis James has called the "Blessed Alliance." She notes that, "Our identity and flourishing as human beings hinge on the Blessed Alliance. God created us to need each other. Male/female relationships are designed to enable us to become our best selves."[5] An alliance makes men and women allies, not adversaries. And in some mysterious way (a right-brain activity?), as we work, lead, and minister together, we give the world a clearer and more complete vision of the God whose image we bear.

WE ARE CALLED TO BE IMAGE-BEARERS

The foundational biblical truth about who we are as human beings is that we are made in the image of God:

> So God created human beings in his own image. In the image of God he created them; male and female he created them. (GENESIS 1:27)

It's a truth that sometimes gets lost in disagreements about what men and women are created to do or are allowed to do in the church and in ministry. However, it is in living out this foundational truth—in being image bearers of God—that we find our shared purpose and our calling. Paul put it this way in his letter to the Ephesians:

> Imitate God, therefore, in everything you do, because you are his dear children. Live a life filled with love, following

the example of Christ. He loved us and offered himself as a sacrifice for us. (EPHESIANS 5:1–2)

In another letter, the apostle spelled out how we bear the image of God in these words:

Make me truly happy by agreeing wholeheartedly with each other, loving one another, and working together with one mind and purpose.

Don't be selfish; don't try to impress others. Be humble, thinking of others as better than yourselves. Don't look out only for your own interests, but take an interest in others, too.

You must have the same attitude that Christ Jesus had. Though he was God, he did not think of equality with God as something to cling to. Instead, he gave up his divine privileges; he took the humble position of a slave and was born as a human being. When he appeared in human form, he humbled himself in obedience to God and died a criminal's death on a cross. (PHILIPPIANS 2:2–8)

We bear the image of God in our world when we follow the example of God the Son, Jesus Christ.

When God calls us to work together for Christ and his Kingdom, that call reflects the way in which the persons of our triune God—the Trinity—work together. We catch a glimpse of these three persons at work from the very beginning of Creation: *God* created the heavens and the earth (Genesis 1:1), as the *Word* spoke everything into existence (John 1:1–4), and the *Spirit* hovered over the surface of the waters (Genesis 1:2). The invisible God became visible in Jesus, and Jesus's promise to be with us to the end of the age

(Matthew 28:20) is realized in our lives as the Holy Spirit guides us into truth (John 16:13). That's how God created the foundation of our identity and calling as his image bearers. Our part is to live out that identity and calling—in life and in ministry—by recognizing our need for one another and working together with one mind and purpose.

PHILEMON AND APPHIA MODEL GOD'S INTENTION FOR SHARED MINISTRY

Just as it takes two to enjoy a teeter-totter, it takes men and women working together to discover the fullness of joy in being image bearers together of our triune God—that's what it means to function as the Blessed Alliance. If we insist on spending our time on a swing or slide alone, we miss the blessing that comes from a mutual and balanced exchange. In ministry, that means we miss out on the delight and greater potential impact of pooling our resources, of "thinking the same thing in the Lord," as the apostle Paul might say. We were created to work together. Women as "helpers" are not merely spectators on the sideline, occasionally called on to provide secondary assistance to a man. Women are men's *ezer*, their help, bringing to their shared mandate what a man needs but cannot do on his own. Functioning together as God's image, they bring both detailed analysis and an awareness of the larger context to their tasks. God made us in ways that call for this pooling of our unique gifts for the greater blessing of others through the ministry we each have been given.

This is not to say that we don't have individual tasks or that we can't make any move without consulting the other.

That's not what this is about. It's about men recognizing the value that women can uniquely bring, just as women recognize the value that men uniquely bring. Here we're not talking about women taking on secondary tasks to support the work of men, or doing tasks traditionally considered "women's work." Instead, this is about our joint responsibility for stewarding God's earth, combining our unique abilities for the best outcome. It's also about mutual respect and appreciation. These are the basic requirements for any working relationship. Without them, the unique gifts God has put into the brains of men and women will not be joined in fruitful ways in ministry. But with respect and appreciation, the Blessed Alliance can flourish, and God's people will benefit from that marriage of minds in ministry.

The Blessed Alliance exists wherever men and women join forces for Christ and his Kingdom. When Lydia joined Paul in starting churches in Philippi, that was a Blessed Alliance. When Mary Magdalene, Joanna, Susanna and many other women joined Jesus's band, that was a Blessed Alliance. When Andronicus and Junia joined Peter in church-planting in Rome, that, too, was a Blessed Alliance. When men and women today recognize the importance of joining our gifts and perspectives together for more effective ministry, that, too, is a Blessed Alliance. When we acknowledge what we each bring to the table *and* what we each lack that another can bring, we begin a Blessed Alliance. That was God's idea in the beginning, and it is still his goal for those of us who endeavor to bear his image today.

• • •

QUESTIONS FOR PERSONAL REFLECTION OR GROUP DISCUSSION

1. The same Hebrew word that describes Eve as a "helper" (*ezer*) also refers to God who is our "help." How does this understanding of what it means that Eve was a helper (*ezer*) influence your own understanding—both of her role and of any implications it may have for men and women in the church today?

2. Overall, did the findings about the differing brain physiologies of men and women support or challenge your own views about the general differences between how men and women think? What recent experiences have you had of "thinking differently" from a man (a coworker, friend, family member, etc.)? In what ways did each of you exemplify or fail to exemplify the characteristics of male/female brain physiology?

3. In a Blessed Alliance, men and women take joint responsibility for stewarding God's earth and combining their unique abilities for the best outcome. What experiences have you had or have you witnessed in others that you would characterize as a Blessed Alliance? How would you describe the unique contributions of the men and the women in that situation, as well as the fruitfulness of the collaboration?

4. In what ways, if any, do you wish you could experience a Blessed Alliance in your life or ministry? Share the reasons for your response.

12

Sometimes God's Spirit Guides Women into Ministry Leadership

In the preceding chapters, we've explored the ministry work of women in various New Testament churches that, in a number of cases, would seem to legitimize the role of women as leaders in the church. And yet, in the same New Testament letters that describe and affirm these women, we find statements that also seem to contradict the legitimacy of their leadership. In fact, in two of his letters, the apostle Paul makes comments that seem to forbid it. We cannot end this book without taking a serious look at those comments that have for nearly two thousand years made it difficult for women to bring their gifts for leading or teaching to their churches. But before we dive directly into those two statements, it's important to review two of the "rules of the road" for reading and understanding the Bible.

Two Principles for Interpreting Biblical Texts

Whenever we come to God's Word, we must bring to our reading two principles to guide our interpretation of the biblical text.

PRINCIPLE 1: *We must use the context of the text to interpret the text.* Some Bible scholars like to put that principle succinctly: "Context is king." The context rules how we interpret any verse in the Bible. Scholars also remind us that "a text without its context is merely a pretext" for whatever a person wants it to say. So the context of any verse in the Bible is crucial to understanding its meaning.

Every verse in the Bible has a number of contexts. These include the immediate context of the verse in the Bible itself, the broader historical and cultural context, and also the linguistic context. The immediate context includes the verses and chapters that surround the verse we're interpreting. To understand the immediate context, we must identify not only the overall theme of the book or chapter, but also the point the author is making in that context. So we examine the verses or chapters immediately before and after the verse under scrutiny.

The historical and cultural contexts take into account the time and place in which the passage was written. In considering New Testament texts, Christians often unwittingly assume that people in the first-century Roman world thought or expressed themselves just as we think and express ourselves today. This mistake can gravely mislead us in our interpretation of a text. The first-century world of the Roman Empire was not only a complex and diverse culture, but also a radically different one from our world today.

We cannot impose twenty-first-century Western culture on two-thousand-year-old texts from the Roman Empire and hope to understand them accurately. In order to understand what the authors of the biblical texts are trying to say, we have to interpret what they wrote in light of what we know about their own history and culture.

The linguistic context focuses on understanding the meaning of the Hebrew (Old Testament) or Greek (New Testament) words at the time they were originally written. Words morph in their meanings over time, which means, for example, that we have to be careful not impose a twenty-first-century meaning of a Greek word onto a first-century text. We must work to discover what words meant at the time the author wrote them, not how they might have been used centuries or even millennia later.

PRINCIPLE 2: *We must interpret individual texts in light of the full testimony of the entire Bible.* At times, a statement made in a particular situation is at odds with the overall teachings of Scripture. We must be careful not to declare a text universal and eternal when it is otherwise at odds with the overall message of the Bible. For example, nineteenth-century advocates for slavery referenced a portion of Paul's letter to Philemon, in which he sends the slave Onesimus back to his owner, as proof that slavery was biblical. However, they ignored other texts in the Bible that prohibit slavery, such as, "Anyone who kidnaps someone is to be put to death, whether the victim has been sold or is still in the kidnapper's possession" (Exodus 21:16 NIV), or Paul's note to Timothy that characterizes slave dealers as being among those who are "lawbreakers and rebellious . . . ungodly and sinful" (1 Timothy 1:9–10).

Part of understanding Paul's letter to Philemon entails some knowledge of slavery in the first century. Scholars remind us that probably a third of all people were slaves, but Paul did not make a point of trying to overturn slavery as a practice in the Roman Empire. Nineteenth-century slave owners used that as proof that Paul *approved* of the practice. In response, we would say, no, this is not evidence that Paul supported slavery. However, he could not change every bad practice in his day; he had to keep his eye on the ball, namely the salvation of all who would believe. At the same time, he would expect that God's upside-down Kingdom would work on issues like slavery, and in the end would demolish it.

With these principles in mind, let's turn to the two texts that have been used over the centuries to make the case that only men could be in church leadership.

TEXT 1: "I do not let women teach men or have authority over them. Let them listen quietly." (1 Timothy 2:12)

Without a doubt, this verse looks like a clear prohibition for all women in all places at all times. How could it be understood in any other way? But let's apply our principles of interpretation and see what we find.

First, let's consider the context. We know that Paul had spent three years (with Priscilla and Aquila) starting churches in the Turkish city of Ephesus (Acts 20:18ff). These were difficult years, but from Paul's letter to the Ephesians, we can conclude that the churches there got off to a good start. However, years later on his way through the region, Paul met with the Ephesian elders, telling them:

Guard yourselves and God's people. . . . I know that false teachers, like vicious wolves, will come in among you after I leave, not sparing the flock. Even some men from your own group will rise up and distort the truth in order to draw a following. Watch out! (ACTS 20:28–31)

As we noted in chapter 9, in spite of that clear warning, what Paul predicted eventually came to pass. From the overriding content of Paul's first letter to Timothy, it is clear that the churches in Ephesus were now rife with heresy and apostasy. To deal with that precarious situation, Paul sent young Timothy to Ephesus to clean up the mess. *The central purpose of this letter from Paul to Timothy is to advise him how to deal with the perpetrators of the various heresies in Ephesus.* You may recall that Timothy was to "stop those whose teaching is contrary to the truth. Don't let them waste their time in endless discussion of myths and spiritual pedigrees" (1 Timothy 1:3–4). Later in the letter, Paul warns Timothy about those who "follow deceptive spirits and teachings that come from demons" (1 Timothy 4:1) and warns of some young widows, "I am afraid that some of them have already gone astray and now follow Satan" (1 Timothy 5:15). The final words of the letter come back to the same problem: "Avoid godless, foolish discussions with those who oppose you with their so-called knowledge. Some people have wandered from the faith by following such foolishness" (1 Timothy 6:20–21). This, then, is the wider context of 1 Timothy 2:12, which is Paul's overriding concern about the heresies now destroying the churches in Ephesus.

The immediate context of Paul's statement is the whole of chapter 2, in which Paul laid down four things that the Ephesian Christians should do:

1. They were to "pray for all people" (1 Timothy 2:1).
2. The men were to pray "free from anger and controversy" (verse 8).
3. The women were to "to be modest in their appearance" and demonstrate their devotion to God "by the good things they do" (verses 9–10).
4. "A woman should learn quietly and submissively," which is the posture of a genuine disciple (verse 11).

The translation of this last statement in verse 11 misses the emphasis Paul gave it. In the entire chapter, this is the only time Paul used the imperative form of the verb. He means to convey this: A woman *must* learn. In other words, learning is not optional. In verse 14, Paul will talk about Eve being deceived because her educational formation about the tree in the center of the garden was not as complete as Adam's. The women of Ephesus, like Eve, have been deceived. They need to be taught. They *must* learn. That is the command that immediately precedes 1 Timothy 2:12: "I do not let women teach men or have authority over them. Let them listen quietly." We'll come back to this verse in just a moment, but first we must look at the rest of the context in this chapter. Without it we won't have the full context we need to understand this verse.

The remaining verses in the chapter are translated in this way:

> For God made Adam first, and afterward he made Eve. And it was not Adam who was deceived by Satan. The woman was deceived, and sin was the result. But women will be saved through childbearing, assuming they continue to live in faith, love, holiness, and modesty. (1 TIMOTHY 2:13–15)

This translation presents three problems that must be explored. We'll start with verse 13: "For God made Adam first, and afterward he made Eve." The Greek verb translated here as "made" (in the sense of "created") is *kitzo*, but that's not the verb the apostle Paul used. He used *plasso*, which means formed, as in formation—specifically, educational formation. In other words, God formed or taught Adam first (Genesis 2:16–17) and afterward formed/taught Eve. When we look back at Genesis 2, we see that God gave Adam instruction about the tree in the center of the garden long before Eve was created. Eve must have received her "education" about the tree from Adam; nothing in the text tells us that God separately told her about that tree. So the first error here is to assume that the verse is talking about the order of creation, when in fact it's talking about the order of educational formation. No wonder Paul was emphatic in verse 11 that women *must* learn the truth.

While the remainder of verse 13 speaks about Eve's deception and the resulting sin of eating fruit from the forbidden tree, it is Adam whom God holds responsible for sin in the world (Romans 5:12–19, 1 Corinthians 15:21–22). His educational formation about the tree had come directly from God, and God held him more responsible.

Then we come to verse 15 with the statement that "women will be saved through childbearing." This translation ignores the Greek text in two ways. First, the word translated "women" should have been translated "she" referring back to Eve. It's not that women are saved through childbearing, but that she (Eve) will be saved through the Redeemer promised her in Genesis 3:15. In that text, God spoke to the serpent, promising that the Redeemer would strike the serpent's head (Satan), even while Satan would strike the Redeemer in the heel (Calvary). This promise is called the *Protoevangelium*, the first statement of God's intention to send the Redeemer into the world.

Second, the translators ignored the definite article in front of "childbirth," which makes it "the childbirth," referring to the birth of the promised Redeemer. Paul then switches from the singular pronoun for Eve, back to the women in Ephesus who are exhorted to live out faith, love, holiness, and sobriety. In other words, Eve will be saved because the Messiah will come from her line, and all women who live out faith, love, holiness, and sobriety will also be saved. That's the larger biblical context surrounding 1 Timothy 2:12.

Now we turn to the verse itself. It begins with "I do not let women teach men or have authority over them." The first problem with that translation is that it makes Paul's prohibition sound like a permanent rule, when, in fact, the Greek word translated "I do not let" (*epitrepo*) always refers to a specific situation or occurrence, not to a general principle. New Testament scholar Philip Payne notes that Paul used the identical grammatical structure four times in 1 Corinthians (7:7, 26, 32, and 40), and again in Philippians 4:2. In every case, it expressed Paul's current wish and not a universal command.[1] Here, we apply our principle of listening to the full testimony of Scripture. The use of *epitrepo* in Paul's other letters clues us in to how we should interpret it here. This is not a rule for all people at all times in all places. It is a prohibition for a specific occasion at a specific time in a specific place. So whatever follows is not a universal command.

If we were to assume *epitrepo* indicates a permanent

ruling for all women everywhere at all times, it also would contradict Paul's teachings elsewhere. Writing to Titus, Paul commanded him to encourage older women "to teach others what is good" (Titus 2:3). And he would not have commended Priscilla for teaching Apollos (Acts 18:26) if 1 Timothy 2:12 were a blanket rule. So this first phrase of verse 12, "I do not let," must apply only to what was immediately happening in Ephesus.

The second translation issue in this verse has two parts. The first is the translation of the second verb (*authentein*) as "have authority over." Why is that a problem? First, Paul spoke of the exercise of authority elsewhere in his letters and he always used a different verb (*exousiazo*). We see that in 2 Corinthians 13:10 and elsewhere.[2] But here he chose instead a strange Greek verb with multiple meanings in secular literature but never used elsewhere in the Bible. It's a coarse word that at best can mean to push oneself forward, to be contentious, despotic, or high-handed; it also has overtones of destroying virtue or of murdering truth. In short, it's not a nice word, and doesn't lend itself to translation as "exercise authority over." So here we're dealing with an erroneous translation of the second verb.

The third translation issue is less obvious but equally important. In verse 12, Paul used the two verbs (teach/exercise authority) in tandem, joined by the little conjunction *or*. When Paul has used two verbs in tandem elsewhere in his letters, that little conjunction (*oude* in Greek) has made the second verb a description of the first verb: "I do not let women teach in an *authentein* way." We're not dealing here with two separate issues—teaching and something else. Paul's concern is not with all teaching, but with a certain kind or manner of teaching, one with a certain edge or approach that pushes oneself forward or is done with a contentious spirit.

To summarize, Paul sends this instruction (1 Timothy 2:12) to Timothy, not as a universal permanent command, but as a one-off measure required by the local situation. He then links the two verbs in a way that the second verb (*authentein*) in some way limits the force of the first verb, "to teach." Third, he does not use his usual Greek term for "authority" (*exousiazo*), but instead he uses a strange Greek word with very different meanings, far from a sense of "authority over."

As we bring all of this contextual and linguistic information to bear on our understanding of 1 Timothy 2:12, the bottom line is that Paul's prohibition applies to a very specific situation in Ephesus. Ignorant women were teaching heresy in ways that must be stopped (5:13–15). Instead, these women must learn (2:11) so that they would not be deceived (2:13–14).

TEXT 2: *"But I want you to realize that the head of every man is Christ, and the head of the woman is man, and the head of Christ is God."* *(1 Corinthians 11:3 NIV)*

To understand this verse, we need to consider the linguistic context, specifically the meaning of the Greek word *kephale*, which is translated "head." It's a common word in the New Testament (appearing seventy-two times). In most cases, it refers to our physical head connected to our body, but sometimes it is used as a metaphor to explain something different. A metaphor uses one object to picture something else. As an example, we might say that John is a night owl. We don't mean that he's actually a nocturnal bird. The metaphor means that John stays up late at night. In our text, *kephale* is used in two ways: sometimes it refers to a person's physical head, and other times it is a metaphor that stands for something completely different. The question is, for what?

If we assume our contemporary understanding of the word "head," it would appear that the text is another slam dunk for some kind of hierarchy of men over women. When we say, "He's the head of the corporation," or "She's the head of that committee," we mean this person is in a position of authority. But before we settle for that meaning of the word, we have to do a bit of sleuthing into first-century meanings of *kephale* when used as a metaphor.

Kephale appears as a metaphor twelve times in the New Testament, and three of those occurrences are right here in 1 Corinthians 11:3. While some biblical scholars insist the metaphor means "authority over," other scholars say not so fast. "Authority over" as the meaning of the word would have been rare in Greek literature at any time, and it did not begin to have that sense of "authority over" until the end of the second century. Other scholars believe that the meaning of *kephale* is closer to the word "source," as in the source of a river or as the provider of life and growth. To understand Paul's meaning, we must look at how Paul used the word. The verse lays out three pairs:

> The head of every man is Christ.
> The head of the woman is man.
> The head of Christ is God.

Look carefully at the order of those statements. Arguments are usually built in either ascending or descending order. If we use "authority over" as the meaning of head, the verse would read:

> The authority over every man is Christ.
> The authority over the woman is man.
> The authority over Christ is God.

In order to build the argument in ascending order, the second statement would have to be first:

> The authority over the woman is man.
> The authority over every man is Christ.
> The authority over Christ is God.

However, that's not how Paul wrote this verse. The apostle is logical, and that should alert us that he might have a different idea in mind when he described these three relationships. Now let's substitute a different meaning for head in this verse:

> The provider of life and growth for every man is Christ (GENESIS 1).
>
> The provider of life and growth for the woman is man (GENESIS 2).
>
> The provider of life and growth for Christ is God (JOHN 1:14).

New Testament scholar Gilbert Bilezikian explains how this works:

> Paul shows that all relations of derivation find their origin in God. He was the initial giver of all life. But in *chronological*

sequence, the origin of man was in Christ, the Logos of creation. Second, the origin of woman was man since she was formed from him. Third, the origin of the incarnate Christ is God with the birth of Jesus, the Son of God.[3]

The point here is that Paul developed a chronological statement about the origin of our life and growth in Christ. God began this at creation when he made humanity in his image (Genesis 1:27). Then in Genesis 2:21–22, God created the woman from the man's side. Finally, God the Son was born to Mary (Matthew 1:22). Therefore, 1 Corinthians 11:3 is not about "authority over" but about each person's source or provider of life and growth.[4]

Right now you might be wondering why we bother with such details about a couple of biblical texts. The reason, of course, is that this book is about women who, led by the Holy Spirit, distinguished themselves in various forms of ministry that probably would not be permitted in some churches today. Women like Priscilla, the teacher and coworker with Paul; or Junia the apostle; or Phoebe, the deacon and presider at the communion table in the first century. Because we are committed to the unique authority of the Bible as God's Word, we need to be clear when we come across something that looks like a contradiction between a text like 1 Timothy 2:12 and the work of women whose stories fill this book.

But there's a second reason it's important to explore these textual details. Women whom God has gifted as able teachers of Scripture sometimes feel shut down by texts that appear to silence them. If God's Word is properly understood, such women may then use their gifts more freely for

God's glory. Because these two texts have been used at times to silence women, it seemed appropriate to explore them in this final chapter.

If the first-century understanding of 1 Timothy 2:12 and 1 Corinthians 11:3 left the door open for women to lead in Christian churches, who closed that door? And when or how? At this point we can benefit from a quick excursion through some relevant church history.

THE UNFORTUNATE LEGACY OF SOME CHURCH FATHERS

The first-century Christian practice of men and women leading together was a radical departure from the pagan practices and philosophical notions widespread at that time. The wider culture pushed back against the churches with a sturdy misogyny. Roots of this animosity toward women lay much earlier in Aristotle's teaching that a woman was a "failed male," and that her role in society was dictated by her "flawed anatomy." The ancient Greek philosopher described women as "dark, secret, ever-moving, not self-contained and lacking . . . boundaries," in contrast to men who were "light, honest, good, stable, self-contained and firmly bounded." For centuries, these ideas about women dominated Greco-Roman civilization.

But there were other factors as well. As we noted previously in chapter 7, ancient pagan cultures had fears about women because of menstruation. As their superstitions became more widespread, they affected the thinking of those in the wider culture, including Christians. By the late second century, Dionysius the Great, a bishop in Alexandria, was the first Christian leader to ban menstruating women first from the altar, and then to ban them from even entering the church. It then became a prevalent and pervasive belief that a menstruating woman would pollute worship.

Another factor included gnostic ideas influencing some Church Fathers. Gnosticism saw reality as split into two contradictory spheres: the sphere of the mind/spirit (whatever was good or virtuous) and the sphere of the body/flesh (whatever was not good and had to be overcome). Church Fathers who accepted this dichotomy identified women with the body and men with the mind. Over time, women came to be held responsible not only for their own sexuality, but also for men's sexuality. Church Fathers reasoned that a man, occupying the virtuous sphere of the mind/spirit, was superior unless a woman with her fleshly nature pulled him down.

Among the important Church Fathers writing about women was Tertullian (circa AD 155–240). From ancient times, a classical virtue associated with women was chastity, but as was also noted in chapter 7, Tertullian expanded a woman's responsibility in this area. To avoid leading men into sin, a woman should cover her body from head to toe in dark, shapeless garments so no part of her female form could be seen. In that same era, Clement of Alexandria (circa AD 150–215) insisted that women attending church be entirely covered, including face veils.

Coming in the wake of these developments was a negative theology of female personhood, teaching that from Eve onward, women were responsible for sin in the world.[5] If we had asked how that was the case, the answer would have been that because women can use the promise of pleasure to seduce men away from higher things, they must be kept out of sight so that they can't tempt men. This was among the factors that led directly to the ascetic movement in which many women chose to live the virgin life as nuns in order to honor God.

Although we can't explore in any detail the downward spiral of teachings that denigrated women throughout the Patristic period and the Middle Ages, historian Elizabeth Clark with tongue in cheek captured the Church Fathers' ambivalence about women in these words:

> [In their view,] women were God's creation, his good gift to men—and the curse of the world. They were weak in both mind and character—and displayed dauntless courage and undertook prodigious feats of scholarship. Vain, deceitful, brimming with lust, they led men to Christ, fled sexual encounter, wavered not at the executioner's threats, adorned themselves with sackcloth and ashes.[6]

Did you catch the irony in that statement? Throughout the Middle Ages, two competing notions of womanhood prevailed. One was of the virgin Mary and the other was of the whore. While some women could flee to the convents and live out their lives as nuns, most women simply had to live with an inferiority that heaped all the sins of men on their heads.

Throughout history, the god of this world has worked tirelessly to keep women down. If we were to examine the positive achievements for Christian women during the Reformation, or during the Renaissance or the period of Enlightenment, we would find some hopeful changes, but few with lasting positive effects. The Reformation raised women from being seen as dangerous seductresses to their role as respected wives and mothers, but it maintained women on the lower rung of a gender-based hierarchy, dictated by their natural inferiority. The Renaissance benefited some wealthy women but did not touch the masses.

The tenets of the Enlightenment proclaimed life, liberty, and the pursuit of happiness for all, but failed to include women, men without property, slaves, or children in the equality they insisted was universal. In North America in the nineteenth century women made great strides as agents of change, attacking all kinds of evils in society. But they were denied the privilege of voting until 1920, and they still have not achieved equal pay for equal work.

SO WHERE ARE WE TODAY?

In today's Western cultures, women enjoy freedoms that women in previous eras could not have imagined. Limits placed on us because we're women are more subtle and, in light of what many women in other parts of the world face every day, may even seem trivial in comparison. But that does not mitigate them. In the United States, it took seventy-two years to enact the Nineteenth Amendment giving women the vote, from the first convention demanding it in 1848 to its enactment in 1920.

It's one thing for politicians to hold back full equality for women. It's a different matter when Christians do so. Legitimate limits must be allowed, but often the limits placed on women in Christian circles are built on poor translations and faulty interpretations of Scripture. In such cases, the limits are not trivial when they prevent women from using their God-given gifts. How can that be justified?

One argument is that whenever we talk about men and women working together and leading as equals, we are denying fundamental differences between the sexes. That is absolutely untrue. We are clear that men and women are not alike. God built important differences into us from the beginning. Now, in the twenty-first century, with enhanced research capabilities, we see even more clearly how some of those complementary differences are essential to our united efforts. Because we need each other, we better understand God's intention that we should work and lead together. To hide behind some notion of "unisex" simply doesn't square with the facts. It is the very difference built into men and women that underlines our need to work together as equals: we need the unique contributions of each other.

As noted in chapter 11, God's intention was that the man and woman should together form a Blessed Alliance, a working relationship in which we would each bring the unique gifts God has built into us to complement the other. This was the purpose in creating women as *ezers*, women of strength. Genesis 2:18 was clear that Adam needed a "helper" who had strengths he lacked but would need in his work in the garden. The bottom line is that we need each other. We complete one another. Working and leading together is part of how we bear the image of our triune God. We take our cues, not from pagan philosophers or from some of the Church Fathers, but from Scripture, where men and women are working together in a Blessed Alliance.

What is the role of God's Spirit in this? Jesus promised that the Holy Spirit would guide us into truth (John 14:26) and would empower us to do God's will. From the beginning (Genesis 1:28), God wills that we work together, man and *ezer* woman, like Priscilla and Aquila. Like Andronicus and Junia. Like Philemon and Apphia. God's Spirit led each of them into the ministries that then opened to them. This is the work of God's Spirit. He guides us into truth. He leads us in developing and using the gifts of the Spirit in ministry. From start to finish, it is the Spirit at work in each of us. Thanks be to God!

• • •

QUESTIONS FOR PERSONAL REFLECTION
OR GROUP DISCUSSION

1. One of the principles for interpreting the Bible is that we must use the context of the text to interpret the text. This principle includes the immediate context, the historical and cultural context, and the linguistic context. Which of these contexts did you find most compelling or helpful as you read about the two texts (1 Timothy 2:12 and 1 Corinthians 11:3) that have been used to make a case against women in church leadership? What insights or new information did you gain from understanding more about the context?

2. To what degree would you say these two texts (1 Timothy 2:12 and 1 Corinthians 11:3) have shaped your own views on women in leadership? A great deal, not at all, somewhere in between? In what ways, if any, have your views changed over time?

3. What stood out most to you about the legacy of some Church Fathers and the negative theology of women that developed as a result? In what ways, if any, would you say this legacy continues to influence Christian views and practice today?

4. As you reflect on what you've read throughout this book, what would you say has been the most challenging or the most encouraging thing you've learned? Share the reasons for your response.

Notes

CHAPTER 1

[1] Richard Bauckham, *Gospel Women: Studies of the Named Women in the Gospels* (Grand Rapids: Eerdmans, 2002), 196.

[2] It is noteworthy that God held Adam, not Eve, responsible for sin in the world because God had given Adam the prohibition about the Tree of the Knowledge of Good and Evil before Eve was created. Adam had a firsthand education from God that Eve lacked.

CHAPTER 4

[1] Rick Wade, "Persecution in the Early Church," Probe Ministries, 1999.

[2] Lynn Cohick, *Women in the World of the Earliest Christians: Illuminating Ancient Ways of Life* (Grand Rapids: Baker Academic, 2009), 186.

CHAPTER 5

[1] Anne Firor Scott, "On Seeing and Not Seeing: A Case of Invisibility," *The Journal of American History* 71:1 (June 1984): 7–21.

[2] Kay O. Pry, "Social and Political Roles of Women in Athens and Sparta," *Sabre and Scroll* 1, no. 2 (2012).

CHAPTER 6

[1] David G. Horrell, "Corinth," www.bibleodyssey.org/en/place/main-articles/corinth.

[2] J. A. Thompson, *The Bible and Archeology* (Grand Rapids: Eerdmans, 1962), 315.

[3] At this point Silas and Timothy finally caught up with Paul, creating a stronger ministry team, Acts 18:5.

[4] Philip B. Payne, *Man and Woman: One in Christ: An Exegetical and Theological Study of Paul's Letters* (Grand Rapids: Zondervan, 2009), 64.

CHAPTER 7

[1] Women were also among the ranks of deacons in the Ephesian church. Scholar Linda Belleville writes, " 'Women [deacons] likewise, are to be worthy of respect, not slanderers, temperate, and trustworthy in everything' (1 Timothy 3:11, my translation). That Paul is speaking of women in a recognized leadership role is apparent not only from the listing of credentials, but also from the fact that these credentials are duplicates of those listed for male deacons in 1 Timothy 3:8–10. Also the Greek word order of 1 Timothy 3:8 and 11 is identical. [Male] deacons likewise [*diakonous hosautos*] must be serious, not double-tongued, not indulging in much wine. . . . Women likewise [*gynaikas hosautos*] must be serious, not slanderers but temperate (1 Timothy 3:8, 11, NRSV). Post-apostolic writers understood Paul to be speaking of women deacons. Clement of Alexandria (second–third century), for instance, says, 'For we know what the honorable Paul in one of his letters to Timothy prescribed regarding women deacons.' [fn: Clement of Alexandria, Stromateis 3.6.53]." Linda Belleville, "Women Leaders in the Bible," *Discovering Biblical Equality: Complementarity without Hierarchy*, ed. Ronald W. Pierce and Rebecca Merrill Groothuis (Downers Grove, IL: InterVarsity Press, 2004), 122.

[2] I've taken these points from Payne, *Man and Woman*, 454–59.

[3] Tertullian, *Di Virginibus Velandis* 9:1.

[4] Joseph Henry Thayer, *A Greek-English Lexicon of the New Testament* (New York: American Book Company, 1886), 549.

[5] Justin Martyr, *First Apology*, section 65; cited in Catherine Clark Kroeger and Mary J. Evans, eds., *The IVP Women's Bible Commentary* (Downers Grove, IL: InterVarsity Press, 2002), 644.

[6] Quoted in Payne, *Man and Woman*, 63.

CHAPTER 8

[1] Translations that use "Junias": the New International Version (1980), the New American Standard Bible (1960), and *The Message* (1993). Translations that use "Junia": the King James Version (1611), the New King James Version (1995), the New Revised Standard Version (1989), God's Word Translation (2003), the Source New Testament (2004), Today's New International Version (2005), the New Living Translation (2008), and the Common English Bible (2011).

[2] Chrysostom, *In ep. ad Romanos* 31, 2.

[3] If Andronicus and Junia were merely admired by the apostles, the Greek text would have used different prepositions (*para, pros*) instead of the actual text that uses *en* with the plural. *En* with the plural always has the sense of being *within* or *among* the apostles.

CHAPTER 9

[1] Dallas Willard, *Knowing Christ Today: Why We Can Trust Spiritual Knowledge* (San Francisco: HarperOne, 2009), 20.

CHAPTER 10

[1] These comparisons were drawn from Ronald Heifetz, *Leadership without Easy Answers* (Cambridge, MA: Harvard University Press, 1994), 15–16.

[2] Walter Liefeld, "Women and the Nature of Ministry," *Journal of the Evangelical Theological Society* 30, no. 1 (March 1987): 54.

CHAPTER 11

[1] Here are the Bible verses where *ezer* is translated "help," reminding us that God is the one who comes alongside us in our weakness: Deuteronomy 33:7, 26, 29; Psalm 20:2; 33:20; 70:5; 89:19; 115:9, 10, 11; 121:1–2; 124:8; 146:5; and Hosea 13:9.

[2] Payne, *Man and Woman*, 44.

[3] fMRI is functional magnetic resonance imaging; DTI is diffusion tensor imaging; PET is positron emission tomography.

[4] Iain McGilchrist, *The Master and His Emissary: The Divided Brain and the Making of the Western World* (New Haven, CT: Yale University Press, 2009), 428f.

[5] Carolyn James, *Half the Church: Recapturing God's Global Vision for Women* (Grand Rapids: Zondervan, 2010), 140.

CHAPTER 12

[1] Payne, *Man and Woman*, 320.

[2] See Payne, *Man and Woman*, p. 376 for the numerous times Paul uses this word to express *authority*.

[3] Gilbert Bilezikian, *Beyond Sex Roles*, 3rd edition, 105–6.

[4] Insisting that *kephale* means "authority over" in 1 Corinthians 11:3 creates an additional problem because it implies that Christ is subordinate to God in the Trinity. This is a separate but relevant issue now being disputed among some scholars. Most restrict this subordination to the incarnation (Jesus's earthly life), while others argue for the eternal subordination of Christ to God.

[5] See Barbara MacHaffie, *Her Story: Women in Christian Tradition* (Philadelphia: Fortress Press, 1986), 37.

[6] Elizabeth Clark, *Women in the Early Church: Message of the Fathers of the Church* (Wilmington, DE: Glazier, 1983), 15.

Acknowledgments

From the beginning we—men and women—were called to work together for Christ and his Kingdom. I would not have had the opportunity to research and write this book without the men who, over the years, opened doors of opportunity for me.

My particular debt goes to Haddon Robinson who, in 1980 as the new president of Denver Seminary, took a chance on hiring me to direct the school's new office of public relations. Fresh from seventeen years as a missionary in Europe, I hadn't a clue about public relations and I had been out of the country and away from American culture for nearly two decades. What could I possibly bring to that challenge? Haddon assured me that whatever I lacked in knowledge or experience, the school would provide in training. His confidence overcame my reluctance to step into new territory that would eventually open other doors for me.

Years later, when Discovery House's first publisher, Bob DeVries, was on the Denver Seminary campus visiting with President Robinson, he learned about Bible study materials

I had developed and was teaching to women. Because Haddon and Bob took an interest in my work, to my great surprise Discovery House published those materials as my first two books, *A Woman God Can Use* (about women in the Old Testament and their choices) and *A Woman Jesus Can Teach* (about women in the Gospels and their discipleship by Jesus).

Then in 1990, Haddon pushed open another door, inviting me to join a team teaching the Scriptures on the daily radio program *Discover the Word*. At that point, Mart DeHaan became another man whose encouragement sustained me over the twenty-three years that we worked together. God, please bless Haddon, Mart, and Brian, our producer!

God's plan in Genesis 1:26–28 was that men and women would work together, both in building their families and in governing God's earth. This is the Blessed Alliance, and I have been able to write this book at least in part because of the men who came into my life as encouragers and partners in ministry. These Blessed Alliances have enabled ministries beyond my wildest imagination. So I want to acknowledge my debt to Haddon, Bob, and Mart (and many others): men who were willing to take a chance on a working alliance that God chose to bless.

About the Author

Dr. Alice Mathews is the Lois W. Bennett Distinguished Professor Emerita in Women's Ministries and Educational Ministries at Gordon-Conwell Theological Seminary. She is widely known for having participated in the Our Daily Bread Ministries Bible-teaching radio program *Discover the Word* and is a sought-after speaker for conferences and churches. She is the author of several books, including *A Woman God Can Use* and *A Woman Jesus Can Teach*.

Enjoy this book? Help us get the word out!

Share a link to the book or
mention it on social media

Write a review on your blog, on a retailer site,
or on our website (dhp.org)

Pick up another copy to share with someone

Recommend this book for your
church, book club, or small group

Follow Discovery House on
social media and join the discussion

Contact us to share your thoughts:

 @discoveryhouse   @DiscoveryHouse

Discovery House
P.O. Box 3566
Grand Rapids, MI 49501 USA

Phone: 1-800-653-8333
Email: books@dhp.org
Web: dhp.org

A WOMAN GOD CAN USE
by Alice Mathews

Alice Mathews examines the experiences of Old Testament women to show how you can build your faith, embrace God's will, and live for His glory.

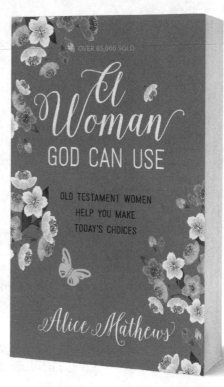

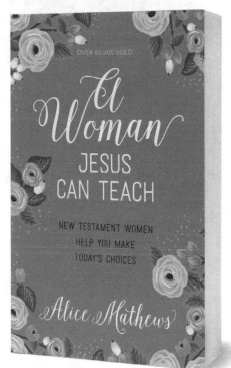

WHAT DOES IT MEAN TO BE A WOMAN GOD'S SPIRIT CAN GUIDE?

Fixing her eyes on the tiny hole, Dorcas threaded a needle and began weaving it in and out of the fabric she held in her hand. She was a woman with a passion for those in need; a woman on a mission to make and deliver clothing to the poor and widowed. And more important than anything else—she was a woman fulfilling God's will for her life by using the skills and resources she had.

A Woman God's Spirit Can Guide examines the lives of Dorcas, Lydia, Phoebe, and other women in the New Testament. In their stories, you'll see how the Holy Spirit led each one in various ways based on her abilities and gifts. Reflect on what God has called you to do as you dig deep into the lives of these women who committed their gifts and talents to the Lord. Discover how God's Spirit can work in your own life to help you make wise choices and accomplish His will.

DR. ALICE MATHEWS is the Lois W. Bennett Distinguished Professor Emerita ⬚⬚⬚⬚⬚⬚⬚⬚⬚ ⬚⬚⬚ Educational Ministries at Gordon ⬚⬚⬚⬚⬚⬚⬚⬚⬚ many years she was a host on the Bible-teaching radio program *Discover the Word*. She is the author of several books.

BY669

RELIGION/Christian Life/Women's Issues

ISBN 978-1-62707-676-0

Discovery House.
from Our Daily Bread Ministries

Cover designed by Greg Jackson, Thinkpen Design
Art by Jung Suk Hyun, Shutterstock

9 781627 076760